Richard Nelson's plays include *Columbus And the Discovery of Japan* (Royal Shakespeare Company), *Two Shakespearean Actors* (Royal Shakespeare Company, Lincoln Center Theatre), *Some Americans Abroad* (RSC, Lincoln Center Theatre), *Sensibility and Sense* (American Playhouse), *Principia Scriptoriae* (RSC, Manhattan Theatre Club), *Between East and West* (Hampstead Theatre Club, Yale Repertory Theatre), *The Return of Pinocchio*, *Rip Van Winkle or The Works*, *The Vienna Notes* and *An American Comedy*. Radio plays include *Languages Spoken Here* (BBC Radio 3), *Eating Words* (Radio 4 and the World Service), *Roots in Water* (Radio 3), and *Advice to Eastern Europe* (BBC Radio 4).

Among his awards are the prestigious Lila Wallace–Reader's Digest Award in 1991, a London *Time Out* Award, two Obies, two Giles Cooper Awards, a Guggenheim Fellowship, two Rockefeller playwriting grants and two National Endowment for the Arts playwriting fellowships.

Alexander Gelman was born in Moldavia in 1933. His family perished in a Nazi concentration camp in the Ukraine. After living in an orphanage he worked in a factory before joining the army, where he rose to the rank of Captain. Following graduation from university he worked as a machine operator, journalist, screenwriter, playwright and head of the Theatre Union. In 1989 he was elected to the Soviet Congress and was made Director of the Committee for Glasnost and Human Rights. After the dissolution of the Soviet Union he became an adviser to President Yeltsin, and works for him as a speech writer. He is currently an editor and columnist for the *Moscow News*. His plays include *Minutes of a Meeting*, *We the Undersigned*, *A Man with Connections*, *Hands Off Zina!*, *The Bench* and *Feedback*.

MISHA'S PARTY

Richard Nelson
and
Alexander Gelman

ff

faber and faber
LONDON · BOSTON

First published in Great Britain in 1993
by Faber and Faber Limited
3 Queen Square London WC1N 3AU

Photoset by Parker Typesetting Service, Leicester
Printed by Clays Ltd, St Ives plc

All rights whatsoever in this play are strictly reserved and
applications to perform it etc., must be made in advance,
before rehearsals begin, to Macnaughton Lowe Representation,
200 Fulham Road, London SW10 9PN.

Lines on Page 2 from 'Memory': text by Trevor Nunn after T. S. Eliot. Text
copyright © 1981 by Trevor Nunn/Set Copyrights Ltd. Reprinted by kind
permission of Faber and Faber Ltd.

A CIP record for this book
is available from the British Library.

ISBN 0–571–17117–6

2 4 6 8 10 9 7 5 3 1

For Larry Sacharow
and Antoli Smeliansky

ACKNOWLEDGEMENTS

Sasha Gelman and I first met in October 1991 in Moscow, the Soviet Union, having been 'matched' in a Russian-American exchange programme. The intention of the programme, I believe, was to pair playwrights in the hope of engendering an interest in 'adapting' each other's plays for one's respective country. Sasha called this 'our artistic joint venture'. I arrived in Moscow with a more audacious intention – to write a play from scratch, from conception, with my Russian partner. Sasha was leery, but also game. In other words, he was very Russian.

We worked for two weeks that October, then met again, months later, at the MacDowell Artists' Colony in Petersborough, New Hampshire; and then met once more in Moscow, Russia. Our play is the result of a very happy collaboration, which may appear even more quixotic when one knows that Sasha speaks no English, and I no Russian.

It must be obvious that our play could not have happened were it not for the help, encouragement, financial support and love of many people and organizations. We wish to thank the US Russian Playwrights Exchange initiated by Lawrence Sacharow, Antoli Smeliansky and Alexander Galin with funding support from the USIA and the Trust for Mutual Understanding; the Lila Wallace–Reader's Digest Writer's Awards for its support during the writing of this play; the New York Public Library for the Performing Arts at Lincoln Center where the play was given a staged reading in March 1993; the MacDowell Colony for its generous accommodation; and the Russian Theatre Workers' Union for being such a helpful host for my visits to Moscow.

We would also like to thank our translators, Irina Vechnyak and Ella Levdanskaya (who may have written more of this play than they know), Colin Chambers, Robert Marx, Bobbie Bristol, Mary Carswell, Gerry Freund, Sheila Murphy, Pavel Gelman, River Arts Repertory of Woodstock, New York, Albert Ihde, and those involved in the staged reading at Lincoln Center: Elaine Stritch, John Seitz, Marcia Tucci, Frances Conroy, Gerry

Bamman, Ed Herrmann, Caitlin Clarke, Judy Kuhn, John Slattery, James Murtaugh, Ben Bodé, Megan Dodds, Vasek Simek, Michelle Hurst, Mary Pat Walsh, Becky Browder, Susan Rose and John Guare and most especially David Jones.

Misha's Party was commissioned by the Royal Shakespeare Company and the Moscow Art Theatre.

Richard Nelson
April 1993

CHARACTERS

Russians
MIKHAIL (MISHA), sixty
KATIA, fifties, Mikhail's first wife
FIODOR, fifties, Katia's second husband
NATASHA, forty-six, Mikhail's second wife
VALERIY, forties, Natasha's husband
MASHA, twenty-eight, Mikhail and Katia's daughter
LYDIA, twenty-five, Mikhail's fiancée and Masha's best friend
OLD WAITER
YOUNG WAITER
SINGER

Americans
MARY, late fifties
SUSAN, sixteen, her granddaughter
FRED, thirty-two, an American business man in Moscow
RODGERS, forties, a friend of a friend of Mary's son

TIME AND PLACE

The night of 20 August 1991 and early the following morning.
Various locations in the Ukraine Hotel, Moscow, overlooking the Russian White House which was the centre of resistance during the abortive August coup.

The play should be performed without an interval.

PROGRAMME NOTE

'The characters in this play all speak the same language, regardless of what country they come from.'
  – Two optimistic playwrights who speak different languages.

Misha's Party was first performed by the Royal Shakespeare Company at The Pit in the Barbican, London, on 21 July 1993. The cast was as follows:

NATASHA	Cheryl Campbell
MASHA	Emma Gregory
KATIA	Barbara Jefford
MARY	Sara Kestelman
SUSAN	Jenna Russell
CHANTEUSE	Samantha Shaw
LYDIA	Olivia Williams
OLD WAITER	John Bott
YOUNG WAITER	Ken Christiansen
MIKHAIL	Barry Foster
FRED	Adrian Lukis
VALERIY	Anthony O'Donnell
TIMOTHY RODGERS	Colin Starkey
FIODOR	Benjamin Whitrow

Director	David Jones
Designer	Timothy O'Brien
Lighting Designer	Rick Fisher
Stage Management	Jane Pole
	Jon Ormrod
	Kath Hoodless

SCENE I

The stage is dark; Russian music is played
Projections:

THE NIGHT OF 20 AUGUST 1991.
YESTERDAY, THE FORCES OF REACTION
OVERTHREW THE GOVERNMENT OF MIKHAIL
GORBACHEV, PRESIDENT OF THE SOVIET
UNION.
GORBACHEV IS NOW UNDER ARREST.
BORIS YELTSIN, PRESIDENT OF THE
RUSSIAN REPUBLIC, AND HIS
PRO-DEMOCRACY SUPPORTERS HAVE
OFFERED RESISTANCE.
THEY HAVE BARRICADED THEMSELVES
INSIDE THE GOVERNMENT OFFICE
BUILDING KNOWN AS 'THE RUSSIAN
WHITE HOUSE'.
THEY AWAIT ATTACK.
THE UKRAINE HOTEL OVERLOOKS THE
RUSSIAN WHITE HOUSE.
THE RESTAURANT OF THE HOTEL.

Lights up on the hotel restaurant and music: a Russian lounge SINGER
is singing a Western pop song, perhaps 'Memory', in very accented
Russian and with great emotion. She is accompanied by a man on a
cheap keyboard. Both perform under ever-changing coloured lights.
The restaurant has large windows (unseen) which overlook the
barricades. Two tables, both set for dinner; one set for three people and
the other for many more. Evening.

MARY, *an American woman in her late fifties, sits alone at the small*
table. MIKHAIL, *a Russian man who is sixty today, sits alone at the*
head of the large table. Both listen perfunctorily to the singer.

From outside the window come shouts, yells and the distant
chanting of 'Yeltsin-Yeltsin-Yeltsin' from his supporters on the
barricades. The singer hesitates then continues the song – even louder

and with greater passion than before. A YOUNG WAITER *looks over the large table – moving silverware, refolding napkins, etc. The chanting gets closer and louder. An* OLD WAITER *enters. The chanting has become deafening.* MARY *and* MIKHAIL *look around, not knowing what to do, or what's about to happen.*

OLD WAITER: (*Over the noise and singing*) Close the window! Close it, I said!!

YOUNG WAITER: (*Over the noise*) Who are you bossing around?!!

OLD WAITER: Did you hear what I said?!! I told you to close the – !!!
(*The* YOUNG WAITER *closes the window. Beat.*)
window.
(*The chanting is now muffled by the closed window. The two* WAITERS *look at each other as the* SINGER *continues. The* OLD WAITER *leaves.* MARY *sighs;* MIKHAIL *pours himself another drink. They look at each other; acknowledge each other and then look away as the* SINGER *sings:*)

SINGER: 'Touch me! It's so easy to need me,
　　　　　All alone with the memory
　　　　　Of my days in the sun.
　　　　　If you touch me
　　　　　You'll understand what happiness is,
　　　　　Look – a new day has begun!'
(*Fadeout.*)

The same, twenty minutes later. The SINGER *and the* KEYBOARD PLAYER *are packing up – the show is over; some time during the scene they leave.* MIKHAIL *is now sitting next to* MARY *at the small table – both have glasses in their hands. The muffled chanting continues.*

MARY: What do you think is going to happen?
(MIKHAIL *shrugs.*)

MIKHAIL: You were talking about your – .

MARY: Granddaughter. She – . She's why I'm so upset. You're sure I'm not bothering you with – ?

MIKHAIL: I did ask. Please. Here.
(*He pours her another drink.*)

MARY: I don't even know who you are.

MIKHAIL: (*Standing*) I didn't mean to intrude – .

2

MARY: No, no – you're not intruding. Please.
    (*He sits back down.*)
    Not at all. It's good to have someone to – . Even a stranger.
    Thank you. So – where was I? (*She sips her drink.*) Susan –
    my granddaughter – she won't stop pestering me. We're in
    Florence, I told you this. And she's met this – man. He's
    American, but he works here in Moscow. Lives here; has an
    apartment and – everything. Nice man. And he was in Italy
    on business. Anyway they met on a gondola.
MIKHAIL: That's Venice.
MARY: What did I say? Venice. That's what I meant. You see
    how upset she's got me.
MIKHAIL: (*Gestures to a place at the table.*) The American man –
    he was the man who was here a few – ?
MARY: That's him. What did you think – ?
MIKHAIL: (*At the same time*) I only saw him for – .
MARY: Quite – attractive, I think. And – lovely manners. In Italy,
    Susan and I both commented upon this. Anyway, it's
    become like the most important thing in the world to her.
    (*She tries to laugh.*) To go to Moscow. She doesn't stop asking
    me. Every day it's the first thing she – . Finally, I say – if it
    means that much to you . . . She'd worn me down.
MIKHAIL: Children do that.
MARY: What could I do? I'm a grandmother. So we have to
    change our plans, take a plane and so forth and so we came –
    for a week, not a minute longer, I tell her. You should have
    seen her face, she was so happy.
MIKHAIL: I have a daughter, I understand.
MARY: On the plane, she's laughing. Everything's funny. (*She
    smiles, sips her drink.*) We're here and we haven't even had
    time to unpack and she says – oh by the way, Grandma, I've
    just talked to Fred – . Fred's the – .
    (*He nods.*)
    To Fred and I won't be needing my room here in the hotel
    after all.
    (*Beat.*)
MIKHAIL: Children grow up.
MARY: You took the words out of my mouth. You start telling a

3

girl like that 'no' and – . God only knows what would happen. On the other hand my son – her father – would kill us both if he – . But he doesn't know. He still thinks we're in – in Italy. I kept the hotel room, paid someone to say we're out if he calls so – . What does he want me to do – tie her to her bed? (*Short pause.*)

MIKHAIL: So – she met a man.

MARY: God knows, that's no crime.

MIKHAIL: And – he has a job.

MARY: And excellent manners.

MIKHAIL: Probably makes good money too. An American businessman in Moscow. They usually do.

MARY: He has a nice apartment. It's very nice. And a car.

MIKHAIL: Then . . . So maybe they will . . . Who knows? (MARY *nods, then:*)

MARY: He's married.

MIKHAIL: Oh. Well, in that case – .

MARY: I just learned this. If for no other reason it was worth coming to Moscow just to find that out. Two nights ago I went around for dinner and I learned – . She's back in Seattle.

MIKHAIL: Separated!

MARY: To have the baby.

MIKHAIL: I see.

MARY: Something about the health service here he said.

MIKHAIL: Makes sense. I don't think he's lying about that. So – it's an affair. Worse things happen. If your granddaughter doesn't care . . .

MARY: She doesn't know. I don't think she does. She was out of the room when he told me. When he – whispered it to me. Of course I've been looking for my chance to tell her. I don't care what I promised him – she should know this I think. Tonight I was going to . . . I'd find some way to tell her – . Maybe in the Ladies' Room. It's one reason I insisted they come for dinner. I go over and over and over what I could have done differently – . But I don't know. And now this – if anything happens – it will be my fault too.

MIKHAIL: No one's been hurt out there yet. She'll be fine.

4

(*She looks at him and smiles.*)

MARY: I do my best, I really do.

MIKHAIL: I can see that.

(*Beat.*)

MARY: It's his second wife. He has children too. None by either wife so far. That's why he says he's so excited about this baby. When he whispered this he seemed quite genuine. He's thirty-two years old.

MIKHAIL: A boy. (*Smiles.*)

MARY: Susan's nearly seventeen.

MIKHAIL: Seventeen – ?

MARY: In four months. Tell me something – are drugs illegal in Moscow? They are, aren't they?

MIKHAIL: Yes, yes they are.

MARY: That's what I told Fred! I was right, damnit! Why don't I stick up for myself when I know I'm right!

(FRED, *a thirty-two-year-old American, enters, a bit dishevelled.*)

FRED: She's still not here?

MARY: (*Standing*) There you are! Where is she?

FRED: (*Over this*) No one's even seen her!

MARY: I trusted you with her!

FRED: (*Same time*) I asked – . She – ! I don't know what more I can do!

MARY: (*Over this*) She's my granddaughter! Don't you dare sit down until you've brought her – !

FRED: (*Yells*) Fine, I'll go back again! Calm down. She's OK. I only came to see if we'd passed each other. And she'd come back by herself. Let me just . . . (*Takes a glass and pours himself a drink.*)

MIKHAIL: (*To* FRED) How did you lose Susan – ?

FRED: Who's he?

(MARY *doesn't respond.*)

We were coming to dinner. She saw the – barricades and wanted to take some pictures. Before I could stop her – . I lost her in the crowd. (*To* MARY) Please don't shout at me! I'm doing my best! (*Drinks his drink.*) You insisted we come to dinner! (*He hurries off.*)

MARY: I don't feel so well.

5

MIKHAIL: Have you eaten?
(*She shakes her head.*)
That's your problem. Why not join me? There's obviously plenty of room – .
MARY: You're expecting – .
MIKHAIL: Who knows when anyone'll come – if they come. What with – . My bad luck for having a birthday on such a day.
MARY: Your birthday? You didn't say it was your – . Happy birthday.
MIKHAIL: Something always happens. You plan and plan and plan – and . . . I've had the reservation for weeks. Two are coming from America. They're Russian but they live – . I prepared a speech. It was going to be very special.
(*Beat.*)
MARY: (*Getting up*) I would be honoured.
MIKHAIL: And if your granddaughter comes – . *When* she comes, she is most welcome to join us. Fred – he can sit over there.
(*They smile.*)
I've ordered the food – it was getting late.
MARY: (*On her way to the large table*) I feel – like there's nothing I can do.
MIKHAIL: I feel like that every day of the year.
MARY: I should call my son – .
MIKHAIL: (*Holding her chair*) Won't he just yell at you?
MARY: (*Sitting*) But if something awful happens.
MIKHAIL: Then it happens. But I'm sure she's fine.
(*A noise outside catches* MIKHAIL's *attention.*)
MARY: What is it?
MIKHAIL: Sh-sh. (*He goes to the window.*) Trucks. I thought for a moment – maybe the tanks.
MARY: Is that what you think will happen? Oh God.
MIKHAIL: Why think anything. That's my philosophy.
(*He turns back to her and sees his guests who entered a moment ago and stand clustered together. They are:* KATIA, *Mikhail's first wife and her husband,* FIODOR; NATASHA, *Mikhail's second wife and her husband,* VALERIY; MASHA, *Mikhail's daughter, and her best friend and Mikhail's fiancée,* LYDIA.)
They're here! You made it! Welcome! I was starting to

6

worry! Natasha! Katia! Lydia! Masha! (*He stops.*) You're all here. Where did you – meet? I hadn't expected you to meet – .

NATASHA: We met at the elevator.

MIKHAIL: At the . . . That must have been a surprise.

NATASHA: A big surprise.

(*They are just looking at him.*)

MIKHAIL: How is it out there? (*Tries to make a joke.*) Probably pretty hard to park. (*Laughs; no one else does.*)

KATIA: What is going on, Mikhail?

MIKHAIL: What do you mean?

NATASHA: What is this about?

(*Beat.*)

MARY: It's his birthday, didn't he tell you? He's prepared a speech and – .

MIKHAIL: (*Turns to* MARY) Thank you . . . What's your name?

MARY: Mary – .

MIKHAIL: Mary. I think you told me that. (*Changing the subject.*) Let me introduce everyone to Mary. That's a good idea. New blood. (*Laughs; no one else does.*) Let me see – you don't know anyone, is that right? Where to begin? (*Looks around.*) Katia? Let's start with Katia – . This is Katia. My first wife.

MARY: Your first wife.

MIKHAIL: And her husband. I always forget your name. And I've known him for years.

KATIA: Fiodor.

MIKHAIL: Fiodor! How can I forget a name like Fiodor!

FIODOR: There's wine on the table. Anyone else?

(*He goes to the table and the guests, ignoring* MIKHAIL, *follow.*)

MIKHAIL: Help yourselves! Lydia, tell everyone where you wish them to sit. You're the hostess. (*To* MARY) That's Lydia. My fiancée.

MARY: Your fiancée.

NATASHA: (*To* LYDIA) We'll sit where we want to sit.

MIKHAIL: (*To* LYDIA, *shouts*) You're not all nervous about meeting everyone are you, Lydia? (*Laughs. To* MARY) Yesterday she said she was nervous. (*Watching* LYDIA) I love the way she walks.

7

(FIODOR *has moved to the window*.)

FIODOR: (*Pouring from the bottle*) You can see a lot from here. People are saying, the army will attack them with helicopters. A lot of good those barricades will do them!

MASHA: (*As* FIODOR *pours her some wine*) We saw some tanks. Nearer home.

VALERIY: (*Joining them*) We're staying here. But from our room you can't see anything. And it smells.

LYDIA: (*To* VALERIY) Where in the States do you live?

MIKHAIL: They're thirsty! They're Russians! (*Laughs*.) Over there's – . (*Calls*.) Natasha! Let me introduce – .

NATASHA: (*Turns away from* MIKHAIL, *and to the group*.) New York City. We love it there.

MIKHAIL: (*To* MARY) Natasha's my second wife, aren't you?! Her husband I haven't met.

MARY: Second wife?

MIKHAIL: One more – Masha! Masha! Come here and – ! I said, come here, dear! Let me get her – .
(*Goes to her, she turns*.)

MASHA: You disgust me. Get away from me.
(*She joins the others; he returns*.)

MIKHAIL: (*To* MARY) That's Masha, my daughter. She's Katia's and mine. Katia raised her.

FIODOR: (*At the window; to the others, as he drinks*) I'd love to see Yeltsin's face when he hears the helicopters coming.

LYDIA: I think he's a hero. I think they all are! And I wish you'd just shut up.

FIODOR: Hero! (*He bursts out laughing*.)

LYDIA: (*At the same time*) All the way up in the elevator, he kept saying things – .

FIOFOR: (*Over this*) He'll pee in his pants!

KATIA: (*Over this*) Please, no politics! No politics!
(*They quiet down*.)

MIKHAIL: (*To* MARY) They seem to be – getting along. I wasn't sure if . . .

MARY: If?

MIKHAIL: None of them knew the others were coming – it was sort of my surprise. I'm curious about something. I want to

8

ask. (*Calls.*) Natasha! Katia!

(*Others look to* MIKHAIL.)

Katia – Natasha. By the way – keep the wine pouring – that's my philosophy. But I wanted to ask – . I was trying to remember when was the last time you two, Natasha and Katia, even saw each other. (*To* MARY) It must be years. Ten, even fifteen years. (*To* NATASHA *and* KATIA) How you two hated each other, and now . . . You see how time heals.

KATIA: We have never met before.

MIKHAIL: What do you mean you never – ?

NATASHA: We met at the elevator. Just now. Except for that.

KATIA: When you walked out on Masha and me I swore that I would go to my grave without ever laying eyes on that woman. It was the only way I felt I could keep my pride. She'd humiliated me enough. (*Turns to* NATASHA.) How do you do?

NATASHA: How do you do?

(*Pause. The group turns to the window.*)

MIKHAIL: What did I do with my glass?

(*He looks. Outside the chanting of 'Yeltsin-Yeltsin-Yeltsin' begins again.*)

MIKHAIL: (*Finding his glass, turns to* MARY) I think you've met pretty much everyone now.

FIODOR: (*At the window*) Like lambs waiting to be slaughtered. All I can say is – it's about time.

VALERIY: (*To* NATASHA, *pointing to* FIODOR) That's Russia. Look at him, Natasha, and there you have this country.

(FIODOR *smiles; chanting gets louder.*)

MIKHAIL: Sit! Come on, everyone, sit down! Lydia, tell them to sit.

LYDIA: Everyone please – the table is ready!

MIKHAIL: I've already ordered. They'll start serving right away.

NATASHA: It's late. They'll want to get rid of us.

(*Everyone slowly moves to the table to sit.*)

LYDIA: I've been wanting to eat at this restaurant for years.

VALERIY: I've never liked this restaurant.

NATASHA: When were you here?

MIKHAIL: (*Over this*) Promise me, please, that we won't let what's

9

happening outside spoil what we have in here.
(*They ignore him.*)

VALERIY: (*Holding up a fork*) Look at this. The fork's dirty!
(*He laughs.*)

FIODOR: (*To* KATIA, *who has been looking at* NATASHA) Why do
you have to stare at her?

KATIA: Was I staring?
(*They are all sitting down.*)

MIKHAIL: (*Holding up a bottle*) Masha, some wine?

MASHA: Sure – . (*Holds up her glass.*) So I can spit it back in your
face.
(*Beat. He smiles.*)

MIKHAIL: (*Holds up bottle*) Who else needs wine?

SCENE 2

The same. A short time later – towards the end of the first course.
Everyone at the table, eating – except MARY, *who has left.*

MIKHAIL: (*Eating*) Delicious soup.

LYDIA: Very nice.

KATIA: Must be expensive. This is an expensive place I heard.

FIODOR: (*Eating*) Not really.

MIKHAIL: It's not cheap.

KATIA: I loved the tomatoes. They were very juicy.

MIKHAIL: Every day they take a truck and go to the country.
That's the only way.

NATASHA: (*Eating*) I should have had the tomatoes then.

LYDIA: How's yours, Masha?
(*No response,* MASHA *puts her fork down and looks away.*)

KATIA: If you're not going to eat – . (*Reaches for Masha's plate.*
To the others) If she isn't hungry . . .

MIKHAIL: I'm glad everyone likes the restaurant. At first I
thought of the Prague. They know me there. I pulled some
strings at work that helped the manager get his car. (*Beat.*)
Unfortunately, it was not a very good car. I thought it was
safer to come here. (*Holds up a bottle.*) Who hasn't – .
Everyone. Who needs . . . ?

FIODOR: I could use some more. I'm not paying.

MIKHAIL: I wanted to – . Quiet please. I thought – while we're waiting for our next course.

NATASHA: (*Not listening*) Pass the bread.

MIKHAIL: It'll soon be here. So perhaps this is the time to say a few words.

LYDIA: Quiet!

(*Beat.*)

MIKHAIL: A few – words. (*Reaches into his pocket and takes out some papers.*) It just seems appropriate – . What with all of us here together like this. How rare indeed.

NATASHA: I've never even met *her* before.

MIKHAIL: (*Over this*) How – special. A very very special time – for me. And I hope for all of you as well. Now.

(MASHA *suddenly stands up, she is crying; she hurries out of the room. Short pause.*)

NATASHA: Where did she go?

FIODOR: She's upset about something.

KATIA: Ever since she got here – .

NATASHA: Something's wrong, I better – . (*Stands.*)

KATIA: (*Stopping* NATASHA) I'm her mother. I raised her. I go.

(*They look at each other,* NATASHA *sits back down,* KATIA *goes off.*)

MIKHAIL: I don't understand. Masha helped plan all this. She was very excited about – seeing you, Natasha, Fiodor – .

(*Looks at* VALERIY.) What's your name?

VALERIY: Valeriy.

MIKHAIL: Why can't I remember that name? Valeriy. A nice name too – like Fiodor. I don't understand.

FIODOR: (*Pouring himself more wine*) You can't figure out women. You try – and all you'll get is a headache.

VALERIY: I never even try any more.

MIKHAIL: Make that three of us!

NATASHA: They're showing off now.

FIODOR: (*To* VALERIY) What about American women, any better? I'll bet worse. (*Laughs.*)

LYDIA: (*Points to* MIKHAIL) Ask him, maybe he knows.

MIKHAIL: Why would I know – ? (*Realizing.*) Her?? I just met her. Lydia, she's an old woman.

LYDIA: Not too old.

MIKHAIL: She was sitting – . Her granddaughter – . She told you all this. If you hadn't been late – .

FIODOR: You're getting married, you two, aren't you? Congratulations. Katia mentioned nothing about it.

NATASHA: Maybe she didn't know.

LYDIA: (*To* MIKHAIL) You were about to give your speech – .

FIODOR: Can I tell you something interesting – speaking of marriage. Katia has often told me about her wedding night with Mikhail. Often speaks about it. It made a real impression on her.

MIKHAIL: Did it? (*Opens up his papers.*) This won't take – .

FIODOR: (*Over this*) A deep impression. There are times when she wants to talk about nothing else. It is like a dream, is how she describes it. She remembers what she was wearing: a blue-green nightgown that tied all the way up the front. She says you had very clumsy fingers untying it – she had to help. (*Smiles.*) And you, Mikhail – I believe it was a silk night shirt cut somewhat long but with little nips up the side. Purple – the colour of kings – I think is how she described it to me.

NATASHA: It was purple.

(*Others turn to her.*)

He wore the same with me. That one time. I never saw it again. Something to look forward to, Lydia.

MIKHAIL: Funny I don't even remember a purple – .

FIODOR: She has talked about that night for years. And when she does – I see how much you broke her heart, Mikhail. How you hurt her when you ran off with – with her. She's here. Right there. This is special. (*Beat. To* NATASHA) I am sure you are a very nice person. And a talented painter, I understand. Good for you. But how he hurt my Katia, the love of my life. (*Turns to* MIKHAIL.) I have wanted to say this to you for years – but the opportunity just never seems to arise – to just slip it into the conversation. I don't like scenes. (*Pause.*)

LYDIA: (*Changing the subject; to* NATASHA) Have you two been married long?

NATASHA: (*Turning to* VALERIY) How long has it been?

12

VALERIY: (*Smiling; amazed*) You don't remember?

LYDIA: It must be nice – (NATASHA *and* VALERIY *look at her.*) New York.

(*No one says anything.* KATIA *enters – no one looks at her.*)

KATIA: Masha says she'll come back. She needs a few minutes by herself. Something – . (*Shrugs.*) She won't say what. She won't talk to her mother.

FIODOR: (*Interrupting, to* KATIA) I was just telling them all about – .

MIKHAIL: (*Interrupting, to* VALERIY) And what business do you do in New York?

VALERIY: I write screenplays for movies.

LYDIA: (*To the others*) Really? That's very interesting. (*To* NATASHA) You never wrote about that.

MIKHAIL: What are they about or can't you say – ?

FIODOR: Why couldn't he say?

VALERIY: I have only written the one so far.

LYDIA: One's plenty.

VALERIY: And it's a Western. It takes place in the American Old West.

FIODOR: Cowboys!

VALERIY: That's right.

FIODOR: What do you know about cowboys?

KATIA: (*To* MIKHAIL) Masha says – go ahead with your speech.

MIKHAIL: 'Masha says.' (*Smiles.*) I can wait. It's important that she hears what I – .

KATIA: Because she doesn't want to hear it. (*To others*) That's what she said.

MIKHAIL: That's it! I'm sorry, but I've been about as patient as I am going to be! I have not gone to all the trouble to bring my family together – for my birthday – to have my daughter tell me to – .

FIODOR: Fuck off. (*Smiles.*)

MIKHAIL: To – go ahead with my speech. Masha must understand that. It is my birthday! I must be listened to! (*Beat.*) Lydia – get Masha – tell her I want her out here this second!

(LYDIA *hesitates.*)

13

Go!!

LYDIA: (*As she passes* KATIA) Where is she, in the – ?

KATIA: Yes.

(*Short pause. They all sip their wines, pick at their salads.*)

MIKHAIL: I apologize for raising my voice. But enough is enough. Still, she's a child for Christ sake.

KATIA: She's two years older than your fiancée.

NATASHA: Is she really? I knew Lydia was young but – .

KATIA: But age isn't everything, is it, Mikhail? Some young people can be quite – . Quite . . . (*Shrugs.*)

NATASHA: She seems rather nervous, doesn't she?

(*Pause. They wait for* LYDIA, *who finally returns.*)

LYDIA: (*As she sits*) She needs a few more minutes.

MIKHAIL: Did you tell her what I – .

LYDIA: Yes.

(*Beat. Suddenly* FIODOR *laughs.*)

FIODOR: 'Fuck off.' (*He continues to laugh.*)

MIKHAIL: So – then we'll wait. What can we do? I can't go and drag her out of the toilet!

LYDIA: Soup was very good.

VALERIY: Sh-sh.

(*Everyone quiets down.*)

I thought I heard – . (*To* FIODOR) I wish you hadn't mentioned those helicopters, I keep hearing – .

FIODOR: After them they'll bring in the tanks – to mop up. I hear they're just waiting.

NATASHA: What are you, a general? How do you know that?

FIODOR: I feel it. (*Smiles.*) I woke up in such a good mood this morning! Nice music on the radio. Sometimes you have to remind yourself – patience pays off. Give them enough rope – .

NATASHA: I don't know what you're talking about. What's happening is a disaster.

FIODOR: Not in my opinion!

LYDIA: Then keep your opinion to yourself!

FIODOR: So much for democracy!!

VALERIY: You wouldn't know democracy if it – .

FIODOR: (*Yells*) I've never even met you before!!!

MIKHAIL: (*Over this*) Stop it! Stop it!
>
> (*They quiet down. Beat.*)
>
> What do any of us know. Look at me. What do I know? I can't even get my daughter out of the toilet. Let's talk about something else.

NATASHA: So Katia, you liked the tomatoes.

VALERIY: (*To* MIKHAIL) Do you still have the purple nightshirt?

KATIA: What nightshirt – ?

LYDIA: (*To* VALERIY) Valeriy, tell us about your screenplay.

MIKHAIL: Good idea, let's hear about that.

LYDIA: This'll be interesting.

> (*Beat.* VALERIY *wipes his mouth and takes a sip of wine.*)

VALERIY: It's a Western.

FIODOR: You said.

NATASHA: He drives a taxi. He isn't a writer – .

VALERIY: Set in the Western part of America. On the steppes, near the desert.

NATASHA: He'll bore you to tears, I promise – .

VALERIY: And there's a cowboy. No, two cowboys. One with a black sable hat. And one with a white mink hat. (*Beat.*) The good cowboy – he wears the hat that is white. And the bad – or evil – cowboy, he wears the hat that is black – except for a little silver bracelet-like thing that goes around it. I figure this is made from American silver dollars. Have you ever seen them? They're this big. (*Shows the others, then sips his wine.*) The first camera shot is of the bad cowboy – the one in the black hat – on his horse. Which is – black. And they – the cowboy and the horse are riding into the peasant village which is made up of wood buildings – just like here in Russia. There's a building for drinking. There is also a dance hall.

MIKHAIL: I wonder where the second course is?

VALERIY: I'll wait if you want to go – .

MIKHAIL: They'll be here. Please.

VALERIY: The dance hall. Where there is a woman – big breasts – big thighs, and she wears very colourful peasant clothes and those old-fashioned black boots that lace all the way – you know, like they still wear in the Ukraine.

The bar of the hotel. No windows, a small table. FRED *and the* YOUNG WAITER *sit at the table.*

FRED: You know what she looks like, you're not lying to me?

YOUNG WAITER: I've seen her with her grandmother. She's blonde.

FRED: Reddish blonde.

YOUNG WAITER: You say she has a camera. Easy.

FRED: (*Hesitates, then*) A hundred. Hard currency. Not a penny more!

YOUNG WAITER: The girl could get herself hurt. I like helping people.

(FRED *holds up the money.*)

FRED: Fifty now, fifty when I see Susan.

YOUNG WAITER: It's raining. I'll get wet.

(*They look at each other.*)

FRED: A hundred now, then.

(The YOUNG WAITER *takes the money.*)

But don't think I don't know I'm being had.

YOUNG WAITER: And thirty for my friend who has to cover for me.

(*They look at each other.*)

FRED: What? Do I look that stupid? (*Beat.*) Twenty.

(*Takes out the money.* MARY *enters.*)

And you better not be fucking with me!

(*The* YOUNG WAITER *hurries out with the money.*)

MARY: What's – ?

FRED: Everyone in this city is a money-grubbing shit.

(MARY *approaches the table.*)

He'll look for your granddaughter. (*Sips his drink.*) It cost a hundred and twenty. I tell you – these people come cheap.

MARY: (*Sitting*) So – we wait. He'll find her and . . . so forth. Thank you.

FRED: Did you call your son?

MARY: I do not see why I should bother – .

FRED: We talked about this. You said you'd call.

MARY: I will – .

FRED: The whole city's going to blow up! He can do something, he's got connections – you said so yourself.

MARY: What can he – ?

FRED: He can get you out of here! And as soon as – as that guy finds Susan – .

MARY: (*Over*) We have our plane tickets – . I'll get her home! I can handle this!

FRED: (*Over this*) For a flight in three days! In three days – !

MARY: (*Yells*) What am I supposed to say to him?!! (*Beat.*) Hi, son, guess where we are? Nyet – guess again. Oh and by the way your daughter's somewhere in the middle of this rebellion they're having – taking pictures – or so she was when last seen, but I'm here with her thirty-two-year-old lover who by the way wonders if you wouldn't mind calling Seattle to see if his wife's had their baby yet.
(*Beat.*)

FRED: If he doesn't want to, I understand. It was just a thought – to save a call.
(*She sips her drink.*)

MARY: I promised Susan I wouldn't tell her father. This was our . . . thing. And – if the truth be told – shy of telling him I have a brain tumour and about three hours left to live, I haven't quite yet found the way of explaining this situation to him without him commandeering a plane and flying half-way around the world in order to tell me to my face that I am an irresponsible, selfish, untrustworthy bitch. (*Beat.*) No, he wouldn't say 'bitch', he'd say – 'mother'.

FRED: Then tell him that.

MARY: What?

FRED: That you have a brain tumour.

MARY: He wouldn't believe that either. (*Beat.*) I used it last year – it worked for six months. No. I don't like to lie. I think people when they reach our age shouldn't be asked to lie any more. Enough is enough. (*Beat.*) What have I done that's so wrong? Six weeks ago – when they handed her over to me – that girl was scared of her own shadow. She was a wallflower! Now at least she has direction. (*Looks at* FRED) Maybe not taste, but direction. (*She laughs, touches his hand to smooth*

over this 'joke'.) Really, what is our problem? Your waiter will
find Susan. She'll learn that we are worried about her. She'll
come back here. In three days, we'll fly back to Florence. Or
Venice. It's on the ticket. Who needs to be told anything?
(MIKHAIL *enters at a distance*.)

MARY: (*Seeing him*) There's – . (*Calls*) How's it going?
(MIKHAIL *approaches the table*.)

MIKHAIL: Couldn't be better. The whole family's – together. It's
what I've been dreaming about. I have to keep pinching
myself.
(*Beat*.)

MARY: Do you want to . . . ? (*Gestures to an empty chair*.)

MIKHAIL: I – . (*Shrugs. Sitting*) I was just taking – . It was getting
a little – stuffy in there. Too much excitement.

MARY: I understand.

MIKHAIL: (*To* FRED) My fiancée, my first wife, my – .

FRED: She told me. (*Beat*.) You're a braver man than I am.
(*Laughs.* MIKHAIL *doesn't*.)

MIKHAIL: Would you like – ? I have a whole bottle? (*Takes out a
vodka bottle from his pocket and pours. He drinks out of the
bottle. As he pours:*) It's like looking at your whole life in one
– one picture. How's the search for the granddaughter – ?

FRED: They won't let foreigners outside any more. They stop you
at the door.

MIKHAIL: What are you going to – ?

FRED: (*Over this*) Someone's looking for us. It'll be fine.
(*Beat*.)

MIKHAIL: Good.
(*He drinks. Pause*.)

MARY: (*To* MIKHAIL) I'm sorry I couldn't stay longer – .

MIKHAIL: I understood – .

MARY: (*Over this*) They seemed like very nice people.

MIKHAIL: Very nice. Anytime you wish to – . (*To* FRED) And
you. I'm paying! (*Smiles. Short pause*.) I left a very
interesting conversation. Natasha's husband – what's his
name? He's a very important screenwriter it seems.

FRED: Screenwriter? Really? You know Mary's an actress – .

MARY: (*Same time*) I haven't acted in – .

MIKHAIL: (*Same time*) An actress, I didn't – . I should have
    guessed.
MARY: I haven't made a movie in – .
MIKHAIL: (*Same time*) Maybe I saw one of your . . .
    (*Beat.*)
MARY: I doubt it.
MIKHAIL: Maybe.
    (*He drinks. Short pause.*)
MARY: (*To* FRED) Mikhail sells cars, isn't that what you – ?
MIKHAIL: (*Smiling*) No, no, no! I don't sell cars. I am the chief
    manager of the automobile museum.
MARY: Really?
    (*Beat.*)
MIKHAIL: It's a good job. (*Beat.*) Any time you might wish to
    see – .
MARY: Thank you.
    (MIKHAIL, *his mind back in the restaurant, sighs.*)
MIKHAIL: I've written a speech. I told you this. I don't know
    what it is about turning sixty, but all of a sudden I feel the
    responsibility to share.
FRED: Share what?
MIKHAIL: My experience. My knowledge. Wisdom. After sixty
    very full years – .
FRED: I'm sure it's a good speech.
MIKHAIL: My daughter's in the toilet. We're waiting for her.
    Then . . . (*Pats the speech.*) She's been in there for . . . (*Looks
    at his watch, takes another drink. Sighs. To no one*) The world
    is an unforgiving place. I say that in my speech. So it's up to
    us people then – to forgive. If the world can't we must.
    That's here too. (*Pats the speech. Beat. Out of the blue.*)
    Never, never, never start thinking that people can't listen
    any more. That they just don't care about . . . The young
    ones. The world will always be the world – no matter how
    much it changes. If you remember things as being simpler,
    well maybe they were. But simpler doesn't mean better. This
    is one thing I have learned in life.
    (*Short pause.* MARY *looks at* FRED; *both are confused.*)
MARY: From your speech?

19

(MIKHAIL *nods*.)

MIKHAIL: (*Continues to no one*) And things being complicated – or messy – that is not a bad thing. Not always. It can be. But a mess is as much a part of the world as anything else.
(*Pause. The others take a turn and sip from the drink.* KATIA *and* FIODOR *enter. As she speaks the other three are startled*.)

KATIA: Excuse me, Misha?
(MIKHAIL *turns, she comes to him*.)
We've been looking for you. Fiodor and I have to be leaving – .

MIKHAIL: Leaving? But we haven't – .

KATIA: Thank you, it's been very nice seeing everyone. Let's go, Fiodor. (*She turns*.)

MARY: Excuse me – but this man has prepared a speech. As far as I can understand, this was his reason for this party. He was just telling us – .

FIODOR: I don't care.

MARY: You leave now, and you'll be hurting him!
(FIODOR *turns back in almost a rage*.)

FIODOR: Hurt him? Tell her, Katia, how this man has hurt you.

KATIA: Fiodor – .

FIODOR: This whole thing is his trick! She's been made a fool of!! If he wanted to celebrate sixty years of his selfishness, his vanity, of the pain he has caused us – sixty years of desertion –
(KATIA *is pulling him away*)
of his philandering, of his lies, his cheating –
(*They are off;* FIODOR *is still yelling*)
– his cheapness! Then I'd understand!!!!!
(*They are gone.* MIKHAIL *stands up*.)

MIKHAIL: I better – . Maybe others are leaving . . . On second thought, perhaps I'll take a walk first. Get some air. Excuse me. (*He starts to go, looks far ahead and stops, turns back*.) It's raining harder. So much for Fiodor's helicopters. They'll never fly them in this weather. They'll just bring in the tanks now. (*He goes*.)

MARY: Poor man. It's all falling apart for him. All of his plans, his dreams. I'll bet they're all leaving. It wasn't a very happy group.

20

FRED: Tanks. You heard him. Call your son.

MARY: (*Ignoring him*) I really understand what he's trying to do. You reach a certain age and . . . (*Sips.*) He looked quite ill when he left. If only there was something we could do.

FRED: Mary, please call. Your son will understand.

MARY: Something I could say to them. (*She sips.*)

SCENE 4

The restaurant. Moments later. MARY *is in the middle of conversation with* KATIA, LYDIA *and* NATASHA. FIODOR *and* VALERIY *are at the window, though they are listening to what* MARY *has been saying.* FRED *is at a distance. Outside the muffled chanting and shouting from the barricades continues. Outside, occasional cracks of thunder, as the rain continues to pour down.*

KATIA: (*To* MARY) Mikhail is – dying?

MARY: And I gather – he hasn't much time.

LYDIA: Misha – dying?

MARY: I thought you knew. I thought that's why – . (*Turns to* NATASHA) You've come all the way from America. I didn't mean to – .

FIODOR: (*To the crowd outside*) Shut up, you idiots! I can't hear myself think!

KATIA: I don't know what to say. It makes sense, doesn't it? This party – inviting us – . Not telling us who else – . I couldn't figure out what he was doing – . It wasn't to insult us at all.

FIODOR: (*Going to* KATIA) Come on, get your purse – we said we were leaving. This is getting too crazy for me.

KATIA: I'm not going anywhere. If Mikhail's dying, I want to see him.

FRED: (*Pointing*) He was taking a walk – .

FIODOR: (*Over this*) I want to see him dead too! But, unfortunately, I don't believe any of this. It's one more lie out of the man's mouth. Let's go.

LYDIA: He didn't tell us – he told her.

KATIA: And how did he know she was going to tell us?

MARY: I'm sorry, I shouldn't have said – .

LYDIA: Masha. I should tell Masha.

KATIA: That was my first thought too. He's her father.

NATASHA: I'll go.

KATIA: I'm her mother – I'll be the one to tell her her father's dying.

LYDIA: I'm telling her! It was my idea *and* I'm her best friend!
(LYDIA *hurries out.*)

VALERIY: (*To* FIODOR) I didn't understand that.

FIODOR: What is he supposed to be dying from? Or doesn't he know. (*Laughs.*)

MARY: From? What was it? Me and medical terms. (*Turns to* FRED.) Do you remember?

FRED: I – . I wasn't there when he – .

KATIA: He looked ill to me. The moment I saw him I thought – something's wrong.

MARY: It's a – tumour!

NATASHA: Oh God.

MARY: In the brain.

NATASHA: I could tell on the phone. That's why I insisted on coming. I didn't want to say that before.

VALERIY: You never said – .

NATASHA: It was a feeling. You think I tell you all my feelings?

KATIA: We must have seemed to him like we didn't care.

FIODOR: We didn't.

KATIA: We almost left.

NATASHA: I feel ashamed the way I treated him – giving him such a hard time.

FIODOR: Wait a minute! How is it this American woman knows about this and none of you – his ex-wives, his fiancée, his daughter, you don't know a thing?
(*Beat.*)

KATIA: That's true.

FIODOR: It's fishy, isn't it? Think about it.

KATIA: You really think he would make such a thing up. No one would make such a thing up, Fiodor.
(FRED *looks at* MARY.)

FIODOR: I don't know what I'm saying – something just doesn't seem right. Mikhail holding a thing like this back – .

22

NATASHA: He didn't want to trouble us.

KATIA: He was too proud.

NATASHA: That's true, he has a lot of pride.

KATIA: Perhaps he told her because – . You know how sometimes you tell strangers things you never tell your best friend?

VALERIY: Or your wife.

NATASHA: Like what?

VALERIY: Things.

NATASHA: Such as?

KATIA: I know what you mean. She's a stranger, so why wouldn't he tell her. You know Mikhail can't keep his mouth shut about anything – something like this, you're right he'd have to tell someone and by telling a complete stranger – he saves us the worry. The man's a hero.

NATASHA: I agree.

VALERIY: Still, he could have – .

NATASHA: (*To* VALERIY) Shut up. My husband is dying. My ex-husband is dying, have some respect.

(LYDIA *enters with* MASHA; LYDIA *is wiping back tears.*)

KATIA: (*To* LYDIA) And then there's you. You must feel terrible. I don't suppose you'll be getting married now.

MARY: I wouldn't go that far – .

NATASHA: I'm sorry, Masha. My condolences.

LYDIA: To think he only wanted to give us a speech – from what in effect is his deathbed and we – .

KATIA: Masha runs off.

NATASHA: No one listens – .

MASHA: I don't regret a thing. I think – he deserves to die.
(*Silence.*)

LYDIA: You don't mean that.

KATIA: Masha, he is your father. No matter what he may have done – . What has caused that? I want to say I do not approve of this behaviour of yours. Your father invites you to his birthday – .

NATASHA: And you run off into the toilet! That is wrong, Masha. I agree with Katia.
(MASHA *shrugs. Beat.*)

KATIA: I don't think she understands. She's young.

23

LYDIA: I'm young. I'm two years younger.

NATASHA: And Lydia understands. Look at her.

KATIA: Don't say it was the way she was raised – .

NATASHA: I wasn't saying – .

KATIA: Fiodor and I instilled – .

NATASHA: I wasn't saying anything!!! Masha, dear – you have said he has done something – something you did not like.

MASHA: More than didn't like.

NATASHA: And that is why you . . . And that was fine. Before we knew he was dying, that was fine, I think. But now all of that is different.

MASHA: He's dying.

LYDIA: Precisely.

KATIA: And once dead, no one shall ever again have a second chance to forgive. To say – whatever it is we wish to say to your father – as our last words that he may ever hear leave our lips.

MASHA: I know what last words I want to – !

KATIA: Masha! Act your age! Fiodor, talk to her.

FIODOR: (*To* FRED) I guess we're staying. I'm going to get drunk. (*Pours himself another drink, pours* FRED *a drink.*)

KATIA: Masha, my daughter – you are young, you do not understand the meaning of all this. We live. We die. And that is the end. Except for God. But now if you do not change your attitude, do not soften your hard heart – . I fear you will regret this for ever and ever. (*Beat.*) Do you understand what I am saying?

MASHA: Fuck him.

(FIODOR *bursts out laughing;* FRED *smiles.*)

MARY: Fred, I don't think we need to bother these people any – .

VALERIY: No, please stay. There'll be plenty to eat – .

KATIA: (*Handing the stage over to* NATASHA) Natasha . . .

(NATASHA *approaches* MASHA.)

NATASHA: Masha, you have been like a daughter to me. Or a younger sister. I have watched you grow up for awhile – until I left your father. And now you are a woman. Listen to what I say as I have learned this wisdom through much hard suffering. A cold soul – is attractive to no one. And vengeance, well, what seems to be upsetting to us one day, I promise you, we soon forget all about the next. Take Valeriy, if he were to tell me he was dying – I would forgive him everything. Why? Because I love him. He is my husband. For better or worse. No matter what I think about it. You start to think too much and you'll go crazy. I suppose that's why I'm a painter. I am in touch with feelings, I don't think about feelings. Anyway, I'm getting off the subject. What's done is done – there can be no truer words spoken. (*Beat. She turns away.*)

KATIA: (*Touches Natasha's elbow*) Very moving. I can now see what Mikhail saw in you.

NATASHA: The same about you. I'll bet he liked your – forthrightness.

KATIA: I think he did, yes.

FIODOR: (*From the table where he is drinking with* FRED) I don't think you've convinced her!

LYDIA: Masha, as my best friend, my room-mate – I have to say I do not understand this behaviour. Whatever your father – my fiancée – has done, he does not deserve this.

MASHA: I'm not so sure you'd say that if – .

LYDIA: I promise you I would.

NATASHA: I agree, what could possibly – ?

LYDIA: As your soon-to-be stepmother, I have to ask you to grow up! Let what happened between you and Mikhail be forgotten!

MASHA: It wasn't what happened between father and me that I'm reacting to.

VALERIY: If it has nothing to do with – .

MASHA: I'll tell you if you want.
(*Beat.*)

LYDIA: I don't think we need to hear – .

NATASHA: No, tell us. Let her get it off her chest. In the light of what we now know about Mikhail, whatever it is – we'll laugh about it. I know I will.

KATIA: Then go ahead.

NATASHA: (*At the same time*) What did he do?
(*Short pause.*)

MASHA: If you inisist. (*Turns to* LYDIA) A week ago Friday, my
father came over to our apartment. You weren't there,
Lydia.

LYDIA: Wasn't I? (*Shrugs.*)

MASHA: It was only me and Raya. (*To* NATASHA) You don't
know Raya, she's our other – younger room-mate. Nice girl,
isn't she?

LYDIA: She is.

MASHA: To make a long story short, my father and Raya went
out. And later, she told me when she got back he had tried to
touch her, kiss her and even asked her to sleep with him.

NATASHA: Shit. He never changes.

LYDIA: Look – I'm not upset. So then why should you be? He
says that kind of thing to any girl he – . You know your
father.

KATIA: That's true.

LYDIA: I love his sense of humour. At first you think – .

MASHA: That was a week ago Friday. (*Beat.*) A week ago
Saturday, they slept together.
(*Pause*)

VALERIY: With your room-mate? How do you know – ?

MASHA: She told me – this morning. She made me promise not to
tell Lydia, but you forced it out of me, didn't you? How do
you feel about my father now, Lydia? But remember – he's
dying.

KATIA: Lydia, before you think anything, just know that that is
how he is, dear. He was that way with me too.
(*Short pause. Suddenly* MIKHAIL *enters.*)

MIKHAIL: You're still here. I thought – . Katia, you said you
were – .

KATIA: We changed our mind.

NATASHA: We all did.
(*They look at him.*)

MIKHAIL: Why are you . . . ? (*Noise from outside; he turns to the
window.*) They're ordering everyone to leave the White
House. That's what – .
(*In the distance, loudspeakers are heard, though what is being
said cannot be heard.*)

26

FIODOR: Enough is enough. Just attack for Christ sake!
(KATIA *has gone to* MIKHAIL *and quickly gives him a kiss on the cheek.*)

MIKHAIL: What was that for?

KATIA: Does there need to be a reason? Among old friends! (*To the others.*) Listen to him, how suspicious!
(*Others force a laugh.*)

MIKHAIL: I wasn't suspicious.

KATIA: Sometimes – in life – we resist expressing our true feelings. Why is that? I don't know, but I think it is wrong.

NATASHA: So do I. (*She goes and gives* MIKHAIL *a kiss.*) If you feel something, you feel it. What a beautiful man you are – I have never changed my first impression about that.

MASHA: Allow me too. (*She goes to* MIKHAIL) I want to give my father a kiss. He is after all my father, isn't that what everyone's been telling me? No matter what's happened – what one does – has done – there's a tie of blood. In your face, I can find my own. With no one else will I ever be able to do that.

KATIA: What about with mine?

MASHA: I suppose so.

MIKHAIL: (*About* MASHA) She's smiling. I don't get it – but I'm not complaining.

MASHA: Ask me why I'm smiling.

FIODOR: I wouldn't. (*Pours another drink for* FRED.)

MASHA: Something – entertaining that I heard.

MIKHAIL: What? What did you hear? If it's that funny, tell us.

VALERIY: It's not *that* funny.

MASHA: Lydia – what about you? How do you now feel towards my father? Everyone's kissing him – why aren't you? As his fiancée – you must feel the most – affection for him. Or am I wrong?
(*Beat.*)

LYDIA: I do feel great affection for Mikhail. And such affection does not wither in an instant. Sometimes – what people do – how they act – it is not in their control. And those who love them, cherish them, accept this, understand this – and forget this.

KATIA: And swallow one's pride.

MIKHAIL: I don't understand what they're talking – .

LYDIA: Pride has always been a luxury – to be kept in good years, forgotten about in bad. Living with you, Masha, has taught me this.

MASHA: And living with Raya?

MIKHAIL: Raya! Shit, I meant to invite her as well.

(*Others look at him.*)

She's a friend – . The three of them are room-mates. For their sakes I didn't want her to feel left out.

KATIA: I think it was best to keep tonight in the family. Sort of the family.

MIKHAIL: You're probably right.

LYDIA: Misha is a man I love. It's not because I have no pride that I can say that.

MIKHAIL: I'd hope not! (*He laughs; no one else does. Turns to* LYDIA.) What do you mean?

LYDIA: There are times in our lives, Masha, when life – or death – and its great concerns makes so much else seem so petty. If it's pride that make us – run away – into the toilet for instance – then I confess I have no pride – only love, and sadness . . .

(*Stops herself, chokes up and begins to cry. Pause.*)

MIKHAIL: Lydia? What's – ? Lydia – ?

(*She turns away.*)

KATIA: She'll be fine. Leave her alone. She's . . . You understand.

LYDIA: (*Crying*) I'm sorry, ignore me.

(*Awkward pause. No one knows what to do.*)

KATIA: Maybe we should – sit.

(*Everyone moves to their seats at the table.*)

FIODOR: (*Hearing a noise outside*) What's that? (*He gets up.*)

KATIA: Fiodor, stay away from – .

FIODOR: I want to look.

MIKHAIL: You don't mind if Mary and – ?

NATASHA: We invited them.

MARY: (*Over this*) I'll sit where I was sitting.

FRED: (*Standing*) I should wait for our friend – .

MIKHAIL: Please, everyone sit down! Let's pour some drink!

VALERIY: (*While the above is going on*) We need another chair!
We're short a chair!
NATASHA: Take one from – .
(*Gestures to the other table. He goes and gets another chair.
Another awkward pause – as everyone tries to ignore the fact that
LYDIA is still crying.*)
MIKHAIL: (*Referring to the noise outside, he smiles*) Every birthday
there's always something. (*Shakes his head.*)
MASHA: You said that already. (*She smiles and squeezes his hand.*)
VALERIY: I was talking about my screenplay.
NATASHA: Oh God!
VALERIY: What's wrong? Katia said it was very interesting. She
asked to hear – .
NATASHA: She was flattering you. Katia flatters everyone.
KATIA: You don't even know me.
NATASHA: I've heard. And I know the type.
KATIA: What type is that?
MIKHAIL: (*To* VALERIY) Mary's an actress, I just found that out.
MARY: I haven't acted in – .
VALERIY: In movies? You've been in movies?
MARY: Not for years and years – .
VALERIY: A movie actress, I don't believe it! Make sure I give
you a copy of my – .
NATASHA: She doesn't want to read your stupid – .
MARY: I'd be happy to whenever – .
VALERIY: See, she asked to – .
NATASHA: She's just being polite!
(*Beat.*)
VALERIY: Maybe I should start again from the beginning since
Mary wasn't – .
MIKHAIL: I think she'll catch on. And she'll be reading – .
VALERIY: Then I'll – . Where was I? The man with the white
mink hat – he's shot. I told you this?
LYDIA: I don't remember.
VALERIY: Shot and now dying. On the ground and people – his
wife, his son, his daughter, they are standing over him – .
NATASHA: Valeriy – .
VALERIY: Sh-sh. While he's dying. Watching him. He groans in

agony, he . . . (*Realizes*.) Never mind.

(*Another awkward short pause;* MASHA *has been looking at* FRED.)

MASHA: (*Finally*) Excuse me, but who are you?

MIKHAIL: Who is – ?

(*Everyone chimes in with their own version:* 'I was wondering too', 'I thought I was the only one – ', *etc.*)

No one introduced you?

FRED: No.

MIKLHAIL: This is – .

MARY: Fred.

MIKHAIL: He's a businessman; he's living here in Moscow.

MASHA: Oh where?

FRED: Near the Pushkin – .

LYDIA: Oh that's nice. (*She has finally stopped crying.*) I like it there.

MIKHAIL: Fred's about to become a father. (*Turns to* MARY.) Isn't he?

MARY: Any day. (FRED *nods. Others congratulate him.*)

KATIA: I can tell you're going to be a good father. (*To the others.*) I can tell things like that.

FRED: I'm afraid of Mary's granddaughter.

KATIA: Oh.

FRED: That's why I'm –

KATIA: (*Looking at the others*) We don't know her.

FRED: She's . . . (*Gestures towards the window.*)

MIKHAIL: (*Explaining to the others*) They're lovers.

VALERIY: How do you know that?

NATASHA: And his wife is having a baby – ?

FRED: In the States. (*Beat.*) Because of the health service here.

MASHA: So what do you want – a daughter or a son?

FRED: Without question – I want a son. (*Smiles.*) I shouldn't stay long – . (*Turns to Mary.*) Should I?

LYDIA: (*Suddenly.*) Speech-speech-speech!

VALERIY: What speech?

KATIA: He said he wanted to – .

MIKHAIL: (*To* MARY, *at the same time*) She wants to hear my speech.

MARY: I told you – .

EVERYONE: (*Except* FIODOR) Speech-speech-speech-speech!

30

(They continue as they bang on the table.)

MIKHAIL: It's rather – . How long before the next course?
   (They continuing chanting.)

MASHA: Start it! Begin!

MIKHAIL: Are you sure, I wouldn't want – . I have the speech
   right here . . . *(Takes out the papers.)*

MASHA: Sh-sh!!
   (Everyone quiets down.)

KATIA: Fiodor, sit down.

FIODOR: I can hear from over here. You should see this. Like a
   farce, they got all sort of things piled up out there. *(Laughs.)*

KATIA: Go ahead, Mikhail. We're all listening.
   (He clears his throat, sips his drink, and begins.)

MIKHAIL: Thank you. I can't tell you how I've looked forward to
   this.
   *(Opens his speech and the OLD WAITER enters with the next
   course.)*

VALERIY: It's the meat course.

KATIA: It's the next – . Fiodor!
   (He returns to the table. The food is passed around.)

MIKHAIL: Maybe I should wait . . .

VALERIY: Who's having fish?

FIODOR: I am.

MIKHAIL: I'll wait until . . . *(He sits down.)*

KATIA: Beef?

VALERIY: Here.

FIODOR: *(Getting his fish)* Thank you.

NATASHA: We'll eat fast, Mikhail.

MIKHAIL: Please, not on my account – .

FIODOR: *(Over this)* He's paying, he wants us to enjoy it too. Isn't
   that right?

MASHA: Pass the potatoes here.

LYDIA: *(To the OLD WAITER)* Is this all I get?
   (They continue to talk about their food.)

The restaurant – some time later, toward the end of the meat course.
Everyone as they were in the previous scene except for FRED, *who has*
gone. The middle of conversation, as they eat:

FIODOR: (*To* NATASHA) Excuse me for not believing you. But I
    have made this promise to myself: the next person who
    comes back and tells me how good – wherever they are –
    is – . Then why the hell are they coming back?

KATIA: For a visit.

MASHA: To see friends.

FIODOR: Get a little drunk and then it's all Mother Russia!

NATASHA: We can be homesick and still not want to be home.

LYDIA: That doesn't make sense.

FIODOR: She's admitting it's still her home! Did you hear that?

NATASHA: I'm Russian. I am not denying this. Did I deny – ?

MARY: I think there are many things in America to find fault
    with. I think you're both right.

FIODOR: It's not America, it's people coming back here and
    telling us – .

KATIA: *You* asked Natasha!

FIODOR: I asked her a polite question.

NATASHA: And I'm not finished yet. I'll tell you what it's like for
    us.

FIODOR: I've heard enough.

KATIA: Fiodor, please.

NATASHA: Valeriy and I have a house – a whole house in Queens,
    New York, which is part of New York City.
    (FIODOR *makes gun noises.*)
    That's an exaggeration. A Communist exaggeration. In this
    house, I have a washing machine and a dryer and a little
    room just for them. In the kitchen I have a very large
    refrigerator, with a separate freezer, a dishwasher – and I
    don't mean another woman, Fiodor – a machine. A
    microwave oven – do you even know what that is? A stove,
    an oven – I have a separate closet built especially for an
    ironing board. I have a complete set of matched and
    unchipped plates and glasses – different sizes for different – .

VALERIY: Natasha, I don't think they're – .

NATASHA: Shut up. Two telephones. One upstairs in our master bedroom; one in the kitchen. Two bathrooms; one full and one called a half bathroom which means it does not have a bathtub, only a shower – with excellent water pressure. We are planning to buy a computer; we have the loan, for Valeriy's screenplays.

FIODOR: I thought he drove a taxi.

NATASHA: He does and that is a very good paying job.

FIODOR: So is it in Moscow.

NATASHA: For his writing. Either an Apple or an IBM, he has not decided yet, have you, Valeriy?

VALERIY: No.

NATASHA: We don't have a car – but that is our choice. We are very near a convenient bus stop. I won't talk about our local supermarket, what is available – the choice. Or our TV – we have cable. Or our answering machine. And so forth. I can see already, Fiodor, that I have made my point.
(*Pause. Everyone eats.*)

MARY: I hate most of those things myself. An answering machine? If you're not in – you're not in. A bother really.

NATASHA: Katia, dear, what I heard about things here – you see on the news and it breaks my heart. You hope it's not true, but . . . (*Beat.*) I simply wanted to say to you – should you need any assistance – Valeriy and I have a little money saved – and of course we can make more – so, if you need something, please just ask. Don't be proud. (*She eats.*)

MIKHAIL: Fiodor provides very well for Katia, I do not think she lacks anything.

KATIA: And what I earn at the school – we are fine. Though I think I would teach even if I weren't paid anything. I love teaching. I like children. (*Turns to* MASHA.) I've loved being a mother. I think – to have children – even just one – it is why God put us on this earth. I couldn't imagine what it would be like not to have a daughter – or a son.

FIODOR: Business at the garage is very good.

MIKHAIL: And at the automobile museum – people come in all the time.

MASHA: Once they settle these political things . . .

LYDIA: They waste their time – .

KATIA: And our money.

MIKHAIL: (*To* NATASHA) But we have what we need.

LYDIA: (*Reaches for Mikhail's hand*) I think I do.
(*She looks at him, he smiles. Everyone is staring at* MIKHAIL,
some fighting back tears. MIKHAIL *suddenly realizes this.*)

MIKHAIL: Why are you looking at me like that?

KATIA: Like what? We're – .

NATASHA: It's your birthday!!

EVERYONE: Happy birthday!!! (*They force some laughter.*)

LYDIA: Did I tell you how Mikhail proposed to me?

MIKHAIL: You said that was only for – . No one would ever – .

LYDIA: I don't feel like that any more. I feel like telling everyone.
Masha, you don't even know this, do you? (*No response.*)
This man who looks like such a practical – down-to-earth
type of man, well, he has a very romantic streak in him, let
me tell you.

NATASHA *and* KATIA: You don't have to tell – . (*They stop,
realizing they are saying the same thing.*)

LYDIA: (*To* MASHA) You went out one night. And he knocked –
you didn't even know I was seeing your father at this time, I
think. Or did you? (*No response.*) I guess she didn't. Perhaps
if you had you would have been against it. But I'm sure once
you could see how we felt about each other – we knew then
you'd understand. Anyway, what was I talking about?

MARY: When he proposed.

LYDIA: We were in our apartment. Masha was out. We'd made
love on the couch. He kept saying, 'What if my daughter
comes back, let's go into the bedroom.' And I said, 'So what
if she does?' And I held him, and in my hand I held – his
weapon – .

MIKHAIL: Lydia – .

LYDIA: And what a weapon it is. I'm not embarrassed by this.
And I said – experience, and I squeezed. And he put his
hand between my legs and said – youth. And we both said –
the perfect combination or something like that. And
somehow or other, we started talking about living together,

34

and then marriage came up, and he proposed. On your couch, Masha. It's hers. That afternoon, I got a little cold at one point and put that orange shawl you'd knitted, Masha, around both of our naked bodies. In a funny way I felt that that shawl was like your blessing.

(*Short pause.*)

MARY: (*To* MIKHAIL) Is that how you remember it?

MIKHAIL: Something like that.

MASHA: Actually – I knew all about you and my father, and so did our other room-mate, Raya. Mikhail had told us both. I was furious with him. I thought he was using you. Or you were using him. I did everything I could to stop the whole thing. (*Beat.*) But now I see how wrong I was. How much in love you two really are. How right you are for each other. I'm sure Raya feels the same way. (*Eats.*) Delicious.

LYDIA: We are, aren't we?

KATIA: (*To* NATASHA) You know what's funny? Listening to Lydia – . And how tender a story that was. I think we all agree. But among the women here – at one time or another – we have all been in love with Mikhail. We must all have stories – .

LYDIA: (*Nods to* MARY) Except for – .

MARY: I'm just an observer.

NATASHA: Give her time.

(*They laugh, except for* LYDIA.)

MASHA: (*Laughing*) Give him time.

KATIA: In many ways he's an attractive man, you have to keep reminding yourself of that.

MIKHAIL: Why are you talking like that? I'm sitting right here.

NATASHA: (*Ignoring him*) I remember a time – Valeriy you're not going to get jealous if I tell them this.

VALERIY: What are you – ?

NATASHA: It's nothing physical. It's nothing to do with what Lydia calls Mikhail's 'weapon'.

MIKHAIL: (*Confused*) I am right here.

NATASHA: (*Continues*) Nothing about that. Not that I couldn't. But one time – we went to see a film, I don't remember the film – but we started to laugh. And it wasn't a funny film.

35

And we couldn't stop laughing. We were told to leave. Even then – into the street we couldn't stop laughing. My chest hurt from laughing so much. Tears ran down our cheeks. We sat on a bench – in the snow – and laughed until we couldn't any more.

(*Pause.*)

KATIA: I remember – not laughing, but crying with Misha.

FIODOR: Listen to this.

KATIA: It was winter too. (*She eats, sips, continues.*) Perhaps the same winter, Natasha. Masha, you were – five. And a beautiful child. (*She takes another bite.*) I knew that Mikhail was seeing another woman. We'd been married six years and this was not the first. With some men – you know . . . (*Shrugs.*) It's the glands I think. Then one afternoon, I was standing there at the kitchen table and I can see him telling me: he's leaving us. Masha and me. He's saying: Katia, I am leaving you. (*Beat.*) He's taking his things, he's moving in with this woman, he wouldn't give me your name, Natasha. Not yet. I try to joke with him – this is impossible. A wife you can leave, but there's a child here, whom you love. (*She looks at* MASHA, *then takes another bite.*) But your mind is made up. It's been an agonizing decision. This is why you've been so preoccupied of late, you tell me. Because you'd been trying to make up your mind. (*Beat.*) Suddenly I'm crying. I'm thinking crazy thoughts – how are we going to live? I'm thinking: what are you taking with you? I'm thinking: am I such a bad lover? I'd wondered that often before – with the other girls he's gone out with. The tears are pouring down my face and I'm hysterical. (*She eats.*) He doesn't dare look at me, then Masha runs in – do you remember this?

MASHA: Yes.

KATIA: She wants to know what is happening, so – I tell her. Your father's running off with a whore. A bitch. This woman who is ruining both of our lives. He tells me to stop it. Masha runs out of the room crying. She's screaming in the bedroom. I begin breaking things. You at first try to grab my arm but . . . (*Shrugs.*) Then I look at you, Misha. For the first time since you told me; and I see that you are crying too

36

– weeping – uncontrollably. (*Turns to* NATASHA.) Did he tell
you this?

(NATASHA *shakes her head.*)

I didn't think he would. This weeping – it calms me. I get
control of myself. And I take Mikhail in my arms and say –
it'll be fine. It'll be OK. And I kiss him on the cheek, on
the forehead, on the mouth. I never loved you more than I
did at that moment, when I was letting you go. (*Beat.*) That
is why I never fought the divorce. I never hounded you for
money. Two years you went without paying anything – .

MIKHAIL: I had nothing.

KATIA: I said not one word. Because – I loved you. Fiodor
knows all of this. He's heard me tell this story a hundred
times.

(*Pause.* OLD WAITER *enters, goes to* MARY *and whispers
something to her. She stands up.*)

MARY: It's Susan. She's here. They found her. Excuse me – .

MIKHAIL: I told you there was nothing to – .

MARY: Thank you. Thank you all for . . .

MIKHAIL: Bring Susan back, she's welcome to – .

MARY: (*On her way out*) I'll ask. Maybe. (*Turns to* OLD WAITER.)
Thank you. (*She hurries out.*)

MIKHAIL: Susan's her – granddaughter. She was – lost.

(*Others nod.*)

VALERIY: An actress? In films. What a coincidence – her and I
meeting in . . . (*Shakes his head and drinks. To* NATASHA)
We should get her address in the States.

FIODOR: Sh-sh! Sh-sh! (*Beat.*) What's that? (*He goes to the
window.*)

MASHA: I don't hear anything different. The crowd.

MIKHAIL: I think if we've finished the main course – .

KATIA: I haven't. But I was talking.

MIKHAIL: If most of us – . Perhaps this would be a good time
for my speech.

LYDIA: A perfect time! Speech-speech-speech!

(*No one joins her this time.* MIKHAIL *stands.*)

NATASHA: (*To* LYDIA) Sh-sh.

(*Beat.*)

MIKHAIL: (*Takes out his notes, looks up*) Everyone have something
    to drink?
MASHA: We're fine.
MIKHAIL: Good. (*Beat.*) Are you all – ?
NATASHA: Please, Misha. We're waiting.
    (*Beat.*)
MIKHAIL: OK. (*Opens his speech. Sighs.*) Dear – .
FIODOR: (*At the window*) Quiet!!! Shut up!!!
VALERIY: What is it?
FIODOR: Sh-sh. Listen for yourselves. (*Beat.*) Tanks. Here come
    the tanks!!!! (FIODOR *laughs with glee.*)

SCENE 6

*Lounge just outside the restaurant; large window overlooking the
barricades.* SUSAN, *sixteen, cut and bleeding on the leg and face, sits;*
YOUNG WAITER *stands at the window;* ROGERS, *an American man,
forties, stands at a small distance – all three have just run in from the
outside and are out of breath, scared and soaking wet.* FRED *sits next
to* SUSAN, *holding her in his arms.*
SUSAN: I'm OK. (*To others*) Please, leave me alone.
FRED: (*To others*) She'll be OK.
RODGERS: If you were my daughter – .
SUSAN: I'm not, so shut up!
RODGERS: You could have gotten yourself killed out there. For
    what?
SUSAN: I was taking pictures. (*Turns to* FRED.) I lost the camera. I
    dropped it, when everyone started running.
FRED: It's all right.
YOUNG WAITER: (*Turns*) I tried to get it. (*There is blood on his
    face.*)
FRED: What happened to you?
YOUNG WAITER: I got an elbow in the – . Nothing. (*Turns back to
    the window.*)
SUSAN: (*To* FRED) It was fine until they started running. People
    were even singing. I took some really great pictures.
FRED: I'll bet you did.

(*He strokes her hair to calm her.*)

YOUNG WAITER: (*To* RODGERS, *who has joined him at the window.*) I didn't think they'd send in tanks. I heard – . Everyone was saying even the KGB units were refusing to attack, that's why . . .

RODGERS: They'll attack.

(MARY *hurries in; stops when she sees* SUSAN.)

MARY: Oh God – Susan, what happened? (*Goes to her.*)

SUSAN: I'm alright. I'm fine, I didn't want to come in – . Ow! Get away from me.

(*Pushes* MARY *back.*)

FRED: Susan, she was worried.

YOUNG WAITER: (*Over this, to* MARY) She wouldn't come with me. Then people started running when they saw the tanks. She fell.

SUSAN: I lost my camera.

MARY: I don't believe this! She's a child! She should see a doctor!

SUSAN: I'm fine! Stop it, Grandma! It's a little cut. I fell down!

MARY: (*Over this*) Where the hell's a doctor?

FRED: (*Confused*) You want me to go and – ?

SUSAN: I don't need a doctor!! And I am not a child!!!

(*Beat.*)

MARY: Look at you, you're soaking wet.

SUSAN: It's raining. Haven't you noticed? (*Catching her breath.*) I was fine. I was looking after myself just fine. Nothing was going to happen to me. I can take care of myself.

(*Beat.*)

FRED: (*To* MARY) Do you still want me to get a – ?

SUSAN: No, she doesn't! (*Beat.*) Thanks anyway. (*Tries to catch her breath.*) I liked being out there. Why is this such a big deal?

MARY: (*Shakes her head; to* RODGERS) She's sixteen.

RODGERS: You're the girl's grandmother? Timothy Rodgers.

(*Holds out his hand,* MARY *shakes it.*)

MARY: I'm figuring out that you helped – .

RODGERS: I have a daughter about her age myself. What the hell I was doing out there – we all could have gotten ourselves killed. We should stay away for a while. All foreigners

39

should stay far away and let them work this out for themselves.

SUSAN: In a little while I want to go back out there. I met some nice people. I said I'd come back and see them.

RODGERS: You're not leaving this hotel.

SUSAN: Who the hell are you? I do what I want to do!

RODGERS: (*Turns to* MARY) I looked at her cuts. Wash them out; she's lucky. The camera, I'm sorry, I couldn't save. (MARY *nods*.)

MARY: I think we owe you a thank you. And I'm sorry if we've put you out in any way – .

SUSAN: Don't apologize for me! I didn't do anything wrong! Shut up!

MARY: Her favourite expression, by the way.

RODGERS: I'd noticed.

SUSAN: I'm not as stupid as you think I am, mister.

RODGERS: I didn't say – .

SUSAN: I know when to come in. And I came in. (*To* FRED) It was getting a little – . I don't know. It felt funny. (*To* RODGERS *and* MARY) But when it gets light, I'm going back out there. I'm just telling you this now.

MARY: Susan – .

FRED: (*Interrupting*) Let her be. We all heard what she said and we should respect it. And – it won't be light for hours. (*To* SUSAN) You should wash out those cuts.

SUSAN: (*Standing*) What room am I in?

MARY: I'll take you. You're soaked through.

SUSAN: What room am I in, Grandma? Just tell me.

MARY: Here's the key.

SUSAN: Fred can show me, can't you, Fred? (*She takes him by the arm.*)

FRED: Sure.

(*She puts her arm around him.*)

SUSAN: I feel like a hot shower. How about joining me?

(FRED *tries to smile at* MARY *as they leave. Beat.*)

MARY: (*Turns to the window*) So it's getting worse?

RODGERS: (*Interrupting*) Did that child just ask that man to take a shower with her?

40

MARY: They're – . (*Tries to think of an answer, then:*) Old friends?
(*The* OLD WAITER *bursts in and yells at the* YOUNG WAITER.)
OLD WAITER: You! Back to work!
YOUNG WAITER: I have to change – .
OLD WAITER: Back to work! They've brought in the tanks, it's back to like it used to be! Do you hear what I'm saying?! You do what I say!!
(YOUNG WAITER *goes, followed by* OLD WAITER, *who begins to sing 'Kalinka', a Russian folk song and a favourite of the Red Army Chorus.* RODGERS *has gone to the window.*)
RODGERS: I hate this city. The greed. For a few bucks people will do anything – that's what it's become. The man who was the head of PR for this nation deserves the Nobel Prize for Bullshit. To have convinced the entire world – for decades – that this was a superpower, when now you look at it – . (*Beat.*) I'm in construction. What the hell kind of bombs did they build? Made out of cardboard? Because, believe me, they can't even build a goddamn house right now. It's unbelievable. (*Turns back.*)
MARY: Thank you again. It's lucky that you happened along.
RODGERS: Not that lucky, it took me a good hour to find her. (*Beat.*)
MARY: To find – ?
RODGERS: Mrs Stanley – . That's your name, isn't it? I'm a friend of a friend of your son's. I didn't know this until today – until he called me. I gather he'd tried just about every name he could find in Moscow.
MARY: My son.
RODGERS: His company does business with my company.
MARY: I understand.
RODGERS: Your son was very – how shall we say it – concerned. He'd thought for some reason you and his daughter were in Venice.
MARY: We were. This was unnecessary. He needn't have bothered you – .
RODGERS: I have a fifteen-year-old daughter, Mrs Stanley. And if someone I entrusted her to treated her in such an irresponsible manner, I don't know what I'd do. I'd certainly

41

– like your son – be 'concerned'. In fact, I think I'd want that person – if not actually hurt, then at least jailed. (*Turns to her.*) He told me a little about you. I confess to thinking he was exaggerating. A son and a mother – . But now I see exactly what he means.

MARY: I said – I'm sorry he bothered you. I was perfectly capable of taking care – .

RODGERS: (*Shouts*) May I ask – what were you thinking of?!

MARY: What business is it of yours?! Get away from me! You've done your favour!

RODGERS: Who's that guy – Fred? I've seen him around; I think I've met him once or twice – with a wife.

MARY: Excuse me. (*Starts to leave.*)

RODGERS: How could you let a sixteen-year-old girl out there?!!

MARY: You don't understand!

RODGERS: What the hell could you have been thinking, woman?! She's your grandchild!! She's your grandchild!!!

MARY: (*At the same time*) You don't understand!! You don't understand!

SCENE 7

The restaurant. Music is playing from a small radio; OLD WAITER *and* FIODOR *are dancing and singing nationalistic songs – celebrating what is happening outside.* KATIA, LYDIA *and* MIKHAIL *are at the window watching what is happening outside – noise of the crowds chanting continues.* NATASHA, VALERIY *and* MASHA *together at the table, in the middle of conversation. The* YOUNG WAITER *cleans up the table.*

MIKHAIL: It'll be a slaughter. They'll just run right over them.

LYDIA: Or blow up the whole building.

KATIA: Why don't they just go home.

MIKHAIL: (*To the dancers*) Do you have to do that?!
   (*They laugh and continue to dance and sing.*)

NATASHA: (To MASHA) We have room.

VALERIY: There's a pull-out couch in my study. Isn't there?

NATASHA: We just bought it – for guests. You could sleep in there for as long as you wanted. Until you get a job – an apartment.

42

MASHA: Everything I have is here.

NATASHA: I understand. Believe me – don't I understand. When I left – .

MASHA: You had Pavel.

NATASHA: That lasted – weeks at the most, Masha.

MASHA: Still there was someone you were with – .

NATASHA: That was a mistake. It would have been easier for me if I had left alone – provided that I knew someone in the States, of course.

VALERIY: To stay with.

NATASHA: Which you do.

(MIKHAIL, LYDIA and KATIA *pass the dancers on their way to the table*.)

FIODOR: (*To* KATIA) We're celebrating!

MIKHAIL: (*To* LYDIA *and* KATIA) The soldiers are probably from Siberia. They'd love to shoot a few Moscovites.

(*They reach the table*.)

MASHA: (*To* LYDIA) They won't quit.

LYDIA: Have you asked them to?

NATASHA: If you think, Masha, you'd be imposing – it would be good for us too. To have the company.

VALERIY: Natasha's always saying she wants company.

NATASHA: Someone to talk to. A woman.

VALERIY: It is an extraordinary place. You come back here and . . .

KATIA: And what?

VALERIY: You see how extraordinary – that is.

LYDIA: Go to America, Masha. You may regret it if you don't. See for yourself.

KATIA: She's not going anywhere.

MASHA: I'll do what I want to do. Don't tell me what to do. Anyway, you come too.

NATASHA: (*To* KATIA) Absolutely, if you – !

KATIA: (*At the same time*) Fiodor would never leave, especially now – . He hates America!

VALERIY: So leave him here.

KATIA: Sh-sh, don't say that.

NATASHA: (*To* LYDIA) I left Pavel. And I was crying. For days I felt so miserable.

43

VALERIY: You're telling Lydia how we met?

NATASHA: No one has even asked, have you noticed?

VALERIY: (*Over this*) I saw her on the street corner. She was crying. I stopped my taxi and she starts speaking – in Russian!

NATASHA: Things like that happen in America.

VALERIY: I'd been feeling a little homesick and there she was – like a goddess!

NATASHA: (*To* MASHA) And you can have your own bathroom. The half bathroom with the shower – which has excellent water pressure. Or share it with Katia.

MASHA: I don't know what I'd do in America. That's not to say I'm not tempted.

MIKHAIL: If it is something that you feel you must do – an urge you know you will regret for the rest of your life if you don't follow it, then – you must. Our heart is sometimes our best compass. (*Beat.*) I say this in my speech. (*Pats his speech.*)

NATASHA: (*To* MASHA) What are you now – still a secretary at the lab?

MASHA: I do research now.

LYDIA: I'm still a secretary.

NATASHA: Research? In America if you can do research you've got no problem. (*To* VALERIY) Does she?

(VALERIY *doesn't know what to say.*)

For me it was much more difficult. To be a painter, an artist. You leave your home, you risk leaving your inspiration. Valeriy doesn't understand this. A true artist draws breath from the world that she knows. (*Beat.*) But now that I know New York – it's fine. I paint buildings now – skyscrapers: tall, and white like birch trees.

MIKHAIL: You were too artistic for me. That was our problem. Who used to say that?

NATASHA: I did.

MIKHAIL: Yet art – there is also the art of living. I talk about this too. (*Pats his speech.*)

KATIA: Before I went to America – .

NATASHA: She's thinking about it!

KATIA: Before I went I'd really have to already hate Russia. Or at least be totally bored with it.

44

LYDIA: Like with a lover.

KATIA: You separate from someone you still hunger for – this will eat out your soul for a very long time.
(*Beat.*)

MIKHAIL: I don't plan to go anywhere.
(*Those at the table suddenly remember that* MIKHAIL *is dying and turn to him.*)

KATIA: Don't say that. Be strong.

MIKHAIL: What do you – ?

NATASHA: Maybe you should come to America – .

VALERIY: Natasha – .

NATASHA: Maybe there's someone he could see.

MIKHAIL: I don't understand what – .

MASHA: If my father doesn't feel like going anywhere, then that's that. Let him do what he wants.

MIKHAIL: (*Amazed at this*) Thank you, Masha. You are, Masha?
(*A noise from outside.*)

MASHA: What's that?

VALERIY: More flares.

NATASHA: Maybe they plan to starve them out.

MIKHAIL: No, they'll attack. They learned their lesson from the Chinese. They'll turn out all the lights and attack.
(FIODOR *comes and gets another bottle and goes back to the* OLD WAITER.)

FIODOR: (*To* OLD WAITER) Do you know 'On the Steppes'?
(*He starts to try and sing it.* OLD WAITER *tries to join in. Pause as others watch this.*)

KATIA: (*Finally*) Mikhail never got to give his speech!

MIKHAIL: No, no! It's too – !

MASHA: Perfect – over coffee!

MIKHAIL: (*At the same time*) I don't think it's the right time any – .

LYDIA: Where's the coffee?

KATIA: We'll get it ourselves from the kitchen.

VALERIY: There's a waiter. (*To the* YOUNG WAITER) Excuse me. Excuse me!
(YOUNG WAITER *ignores him.*)

NATASHA: Forget the coffee, let's hear the speech! I've waited long enough! Come on – speech-speech-speech – .

EVERYONE: (*Except* FIODOR *and the* WAITERS) Speech-speech-speech-speech!

MIKHAIL: Fine! OK! OK! I hear you! Fine!

(*They calm down.*)

It seems a little inappropriate what with what is happening out . . . But if you insist. (*Takes out his speech.*)

NATASHA: (*Whispers to* MASHA) Get out of this country while you still can.

KATIA: Sh-sh.

(MIKHAIL *clears his throat and there is an explosion outside.*)

NATASHA: Oh God.

(*The dancers stop.*)

VALERIY: They're getting ready. Any moment.

LYDIA: I think we should all just try and block that out.

MASHA: You're good at that.

MIKHAIL: Should I – ?

(*He means – continue – but everyone is listening for the next explosion from outside.*)

NATASHA: (*Whispers to* MASHA) You'll like our neighbourhood in Queens – it's like here around the Ukraine Hotel, but nicer – cleaner. You'll go crazy when you see what you can buy.

KATIA: Natasha.

(*Beat.*)

NATASHA: (*One more thought, to* MASHA) There's an Orthodox church two blocks away.

(*Another explosion.*)

MIKHAIL: When we are young we want to be able to change the world; when we are old we're lucky to be able to change our pants. (*Smiles. No one is listening.*) I say that in here. (*Rustles his speech.*)

FIODOR: I've got a speech of my own.

KATIA: Fiodor!

FIODOR: (*With bottle in hand*) In three, five years – ten at the most – our children will thank us for this day!! In twenty years, they'll look back and see our sacrifices – .

MASHA: Shut up!

KATIA: (*to* MASHA) Don't talk to Fiodor that way!

FIODOR: (*To* MASHA) It's for you that we are doing this, dear.

LYDIA: What are you doing? Look at you, what the hell do you think you're doing?

FIODOR: If it were up to me, I'd take gasoline and pour it all around the building and – .

NATASHA: (*Upset*) He's an idiot. Shut him up!

VALERIY: (*To* FIODOR, *at the same time*) You make me sick!

FIODOR: Come here and say that!

VALERIY: (*Interrupting*) I'm coming! (*Stands up.*)

NATASHA: (*To* VALERIY) What are you doing? Stop him! Stop him!

FIODOR: (*Screaming*) Come here! Come here!

OLD WAITER: (*To* FIODOR) You show him!

MASHA: They're going to fight!

VALERIY: (*Over this, as he takes off his jacket*) You idiot! You stupid – !

MIKHAIL: (*Trying to stop* VALERIY:) Valeriy – .

VALERIY: In some ways, it's Mikhail that I envy. He won't have to watch such idiocy for too much longer. He's dying. Good for you!

(*Beat. They all have heard what he has said.*)

NATASHA: Valeriy!

LYDIA: Sh-sh.

KATIA: He didn't mean – .

MIKHAIL: What didn't he mean? Who's dying? Who put such a ridiculous idea into your head?

(*They all look at him, though also try to look away.*)

What's he talking about? Why are you looking at me like that? I'm not dying! (*Tries to laugh.*) Who said I was dying? Look at me! I'm as healthy as a horse. As a stud! (*Laughs.*) I've got the body of a boy! And the needs! (*Laughs, no one else does.*) Look at me. (*Beat.*) Look at me!

(*Beat. Noise and chanting grows outside.*)

Susan's room in the hotel. MARY *and* SUSAN *are in the middle of conversation;* SUSAN *is in a robe now, her hair wet from a shower.* FRED *stands to one side, he is drying his hair with a towel.*

SUSAN: Is it my turn to talk?

MARY: Susan!

SUSAN: Is it now my turn?!!!!

MARY: What do you want to . . . ? (*Stops herself, looks at* FRED.) Does he have to stand there?

FRED: I'll – . I'll wait in the – . (*Tries to rub his head faster with the towel.*) Stupid towels they have here. Can't get yourself dry. Excuse me. (*He leaves.*)

SUSAN: First you promise that we won't call Dad.

MARY: (*Over this*) I didn't call – !

SUSAN: (*Continuing*) We agreed about this. We wouldn't even tell him that we'd come to Moscow.

MARY: (*Over this*) I don't know how he found out, I told you.

SUSAN: Right! So you broke your promise!!

MARY: Not that I wasn't going to call him! I am responsible for you – .

SUSAN: I'm talking now!!! (*Beat.*) Responsible? You were at some guy's birthday party! What are you talking about – responsible?!

MARY: That's not fair. You don't want to understand.

SUSAN: It's not me who doesn't understand, Grandmother.

MARY: I understand more about you than you – !

SUSAN: (*Interrupting*) You don't know anything about me!! (*They breathe heavily for a moment.*) About my life. (*Beat.*) This was important to me.

MARY: You're sixteen years old. You could have gotten hurt. Seriously hurt – .

SUSAN: I was being careful – .

MARY: Your camera got smashed. You have cuts all down your legs, on your face – .

SUSAN: (*Turning away*) I really do hate you.

MARY: Don't be ridiculous.

SUSAN: What do you know about me?

MARY: Susan – ?

SUSAN: When have you ever bothered to ask me – about me?

MARY: We have been together on this trip for six – .

SUSAN: That's what I'm saying – you don't know anything!! Why do you think Dad let me go on this trip with you of all people?! (*Beat.*) You know how he talks about you, don't you? (*No response.*) The word 'selfish' comes out quite a lot.

MARY: I know what my son thinks about me, you're not going to hurt me by this, Susan, if that is your point.

SUSAN: 'Irresponsible', 'unreliable', 'a liar' – .

MARY: Even worse, I'm sure. Remember, I've known your father longer than you have . . .
(*Beat.*)

SUSAN: You were supposed to be different. That's why I agreed to this. I thought you'd understand me!

MARY: As one selfish person to another? (*Beat.*) Who agreed to bring you here? Don't you think I knew how your father would react?! Still I did this – for you!!
(*Beat. Knock on the door*: RODGERS *enters.*)

RODGERS: (*Looks at* SUSAN, *then back to* MARY) Did she wash out the cuts?

MARY: (*Nods*) They were just scratches.

RODGERS: She was lucky.

SUSAN: Was I?

RODGERS: (*To* MARY) Your son's – . He's relieved that we found her. I didn't tell him everything. I figure she'll be home soon, he'll see her – . Why worry him about what – fortunately – didn't happen.

SUSAN: (*Half to herself*) I'm right here.

RODGERS: I'll have to tell him at a later date, of course, – if he asks.

MARY: About – ?

RODGERS: I met Fred – in the corridor.

MARY: I wouldn't want you to lie on my account.

RODGERS: I wouldn't do that – on your account. Here's a ticket on this morning's Pan Am flight. It wasn't easy to get. Your son pulled strings. (*Hands* MARY *the ticket.*) There's only one. You still have your – ?

MARY: One?

RODGERS: Does she mind travelling alone?

SUSAN: I'm right here! I'm here! Talk to me!

> (*Beat.*)

RODGERS: Well – do you? (*No response.*) I'll wait – . If she needs help with her luggage . . . We should leave as soon as possible, who knows what's going to happen. There are rumours that people have been killed. I told her father I'd get her to the airport; that made him happy – or at least calmed him down a bit.

> (*He goes. Short pause.*)

MARY: (*Looking at the ticket*) He's only doing your father a favour, we shouldn't be angry with him.

SUSAN: (*Erupts*) I am sixteen years old!!!!

> (*Pause.*)

MARY: (*Quietly*) I know you are.

> (SUSAN *begins to cry*.)

We've had a wonderful time together. I have. And this is only the beginning, Susan. Now that we're friends – pals really – . Maybe you'll come and spend a weekend or two with me in New York. There's plenty there we can do – . Now that I know the sort of things you like – .

SUSAN: Dad – .

MARY: If your father permits me to see you – .

SUSAN: Dad doesn't like you.

MARY: I'm not sure whether that is true or not – I'm not even sure whether he knows what he feels about me.

SUSAN: Dad, I gather – he avoided telling you about how – . (*Beat. She swallows and continues.*) How twice already this year – he and Mom have had to hurry me to the emergency room of the hospital – .

MARY: Susan – .

SUSAN: To have a quantity of pills pumped out of my stomach. (*Beat.*) You see, the reason he agreed to this trip with you is that he simply didn't know what else to do with me. (*Beat.*) He's a desperate man.

> (*Pause.*)

MARY: Pack. (*She stands and looks out the window.*) And why – would a young woman like yourself want to hurt herself? (*No response*.) I'm sure you don't know. I'll let you pack. (*She goes to the door*.)

SUSAN: I just remember wanting to die.

MARY: (*Scream*) Stop it!!!! (*Looks at her*.) Your father told me. Of course I've known. I have sat watching him try to talk about it. Try to understand.
(*Beat*.)

SUSAN: I should have guessed. He promised not to tell you. (*Laughs to herself*.)

MARY: Let me finish. Believe me, Susan, I have sympathy. I do. The world is – whatever. I agree. But let me tell you – night after night these past six weeks I have walked into your rooms to watch you sleep. How could anyone with that much life think of anything but living? This is the thought that kept coming into my head – seeing you asleep. Like an angel. (*Beat*.) Even one night in Paris when you had company. Asleep, he looked like an angel too. (*Beat*.) So much life. Then each day, that look in your eyes – how your father talked about that look; it made him cry. Little by little, it went away. Each day you seemed a little happier, or a little – less sad. Waking up, having fun – the two of us. I can only say – that for me – these weeks have been the happiest of my life. (*Turns to the door. Turns back*.) I did call your father. I lied. So what? I'll let you pack. (*She goes*.)

SCENE 9

Valeriy and Natasha's room in the hotel. VALERIY *and* NATASHA *are packing*.

VALERIY: They'll just kill them. That's what it'll come down to.

NATASHA: We don't know that for – .

VALERIY: You saw the tanks! That's the sort of country we grew up in. Now I see why we left.

NATASHA: You keep saying that about everything – I didn't think you needed another reason.
(*Beat*.)

51

VALERIY: I don't know what I was expecting. I was sort of looking forward to this.

(*She looks at him.*)

I was. A little. Then it all comes back to you. How easy we forget, Natasha.

(*She continues to pack.*)

Out there, it is all falling apart. This is what it's all been leading to. Only this. It makes you sick! (*Throws a piece of clothing down.*) Everything's filthy! Everyone's got his hand out. And now there's the tanks – nothing changes. Have these people no pride?!

NATASHA: I'm sure they have pride – .

VALERIY: It makes you embarrassed to call yourself a Russian!

NATASHA: Valeriy, that's not – .

VALERIY: Compare this city with – say New York. With Queens – .

NATASHA: Be fair!!

VALERIY: Aren't I? Politics – that's what's destroyed this country and may it rot in hell. Thank God we're leaving. Thank you God that we have someplace to go.

(*Knock at the door.* NATASHA *goes and opens it.* MIKHAIL *is there.*)

MIKHAIL: I'm sorry to interrupt.

VALERIY: (*Packing*) He has a lot of nerve, showing up here.

MIKHAIL: (*Continuing*) There's a man – an American. He's taking – someone else to the airport. He's offered . . . I asked and he offered – if you want a ride.

VALERIY: (*To* NATASHA) Then we can take the first plane we can get out of here – wherever it's going.

(NATASHA *has stopped packing.*)

MIKHAIL: Natasha? (*No response.*) I'll tell him to expect you. (*He turns to leave.*)

NATASHA: He looks healthy. A miraculous recovery.

MIKHAIL: I never said I was dying, that was someone else's idea – .

NATASHA: You expect us to believe – !

MIKHAIL: It's true!

NATASHA: One more lie, one more deception out of your mouth – !

VALERIY: Natasha, he's not worth it.

MIKHAIL: Who's not worth it? You, you taxi-cab driver – !

VALERIY: This trip cost me a fortune! Don't get me angrier than I am! The money we wasted! What we could have bought!

MIKHAIL: Call him off, Natasha, before I step on him!

NATASHA: Just get out of here! I've heard all the lies I can take for one night.

(MIKHAIL *turns then turns back*.)

MIKHAIL: Then why did you come here? If you hated me so much?! Tell me that! Why are you here? Damn it, answer me that!!!!

VALERIY: Don't you shout at – .

NATASHA: I don't need your protection, thank you.

VALERIY: Natasha – .

NATASHA: Don't touch me.

VALERIY: Me?

NATASHA: And shut up. (*Beat*.)

MIKHAIL: Well? (*Beat*.) Why are you here, Natasha? Why did you come?

(*Beat*. MIKHAIL *goes. Short pause.* NATASHA *sits;* VALERIY *watches her for a moment, then*:)

VALERIY: Let's pack. We have a ride. There'll be some flight we can catch.

(*She doesn't move*.)

I'm packing. I told you this was all a mistake. The money – thrown away. Poor Lydia – she has to marry him. The sympathy you must feel for her. (*Tries to laugh; no response*.) I hate this room. Look at it. It's dirty. Two lights don't work. The bed – . I hate the toilet paper – I'll bet you do too – . Nothing like in . . . In Queens. We forget what it's like. Don't we? Funny, isn't it? Natasha, pack. (*He looks at her, then sits next to her and takes her hand*.) I'm not going to watch this country destroy itself. I have my life. We have our life. I'm not going to stay a second more than I have to. I'd hoped when you'd seen – . There's nothing here for you, Natasha! Do you see what they're doing in the streets?! (*Beat*.) He's marrying Lydia!!!

(*She looks at him, hugs him. Beat*.)

The electric cords are frayed. The plug in the bathroom

doesn't fit the drain. I don't for one second buy that you
need – . (*Gestures around the room.*) For inspiration. We
carry what we need with us. Your painting is getting even
better.

(*She looks at him.*)

I say so.

(*She tries to smile but has begun to cry.*)

Natasha.

(*They hug as she cries.*)

At the airport, the conveyor belt for the luggage – did you
notice? – it was built at such an angle so that luggage as it
goes around – falls off. (*Beat.*) What sort of country is this?

(*Short pause.*)

SCENE 10

Lounge outside the restaurant. LYDIA *sits in a chair.* MIKHAIL
approaches on his way to the restaurant.

LYDIA: Mikhail.

(*He turns and sees her.*)

MIKHAIL: Lydia, what are you doing out here?

LYDIA: I wanted to see you.

MIKHAIL: We have guests; you're the hostess, we should be
seeing them – .

LYDIA: I wanted to see you alone. (*Beat.*) Are you all right?

MIKHAIL: I've been arguing with Natasha. Nothing changes. I
feel I've spent a lifetime arguing with Natasha. Why I let
her bother me – .

LYDIA: Mikhail. I want you to know that I have known about
you and Raya since the morning after it happened.

(*He looks at her.*)

MIKHAIL: Raya??? Who's Raya?

(*She looks at him.*)

Oh – yours and Masha's room-mate. That's her name, isn't
it? Dark hair – . That Raya? Since what happened?

LYDIA: Everyone knows, Misha.

MIKHAIL: I don't know what you're talking about. Anyway,

can't this wait? They're – . (*Stops himself.*) Has this Raya been saying something about me?
(*Beat.*)

LYDIA: You slept with her. Perhaps still are sleeping with her. I'm not sure about that.

MIKHAIL: You can't be serious – !

LYDIA: Mikhail, Masha told everyone, please! I am not criticizing you, I knew about it. These things happen. I understand. (*Beat.*) I wish Masha had kept it to herself, but . . .
(*Short pause. He looks towards the restaurant then back at* LYDIA.)

MIKHAIL: Masha said this? (*Beat.*) I suppose it could have happened – once, twice, I hardly even remember – .
(*She looks down. Pause.*)
You didn't know, did you? Shit!!!!

LYDIA: I simply wanted you to know that that wasn't the reason.

MIKHAIL: The reason for – for what, Lydia?

LYDIA: Do you want a drink? (*She takes out a small silver flask.*) I was going to give this to you. Why not, I still will. Here. (*Hands him the flask.*) Happy birthday. I think everyone else has forgotten it – was – your – birthday.
(*He drinks from the flask.*)
Sit down.
(*He doesn't.*)
I suppose it was when we thought – everyone thought you were dying – .

MIKHAIL: That was not my idea, Mary – .

LYDIA: Please. I believe you. Let me finish. This is very important to me. (*Beat.*) When I started to believe about your imminent death, something happened to me, Mikhail. Something that I will admit is quite selfish – which as you know is in itself very rare for me.

MIKHAIL: You are not a selfish woman.

LYDIA: No. No I'm not. (*Beat.*) Anyway – what I started to do – was think about – me. And then you came into the restaurant. I looked at you – or I remember thinking I was looking at you – very very differently. (*Beat.*) What struck

55

me – as I saw you for the first time as a dying man – what struck me was – that you are old.

MIKHAIL: (*Gasps*) Oh God.

LYDIA: Sh-sh. Please. Old. I'm just about finished. A dying old man.

MIKHAIL: But she made that up. Look at me, I'm – .

LYDIA: So what? That's what I saw and I can't erase what I saw from my brain now can I? It's how I saw you – it's how I see you still. (*Beat.*) Because – you *are* old, after all. I just hadn't seen that before. I'm sorry. (*She takes her ring off and hands it back to him.*) I really am sorry. And I want to apologize for my selfishness. It's not often in my life that I have thought of me. (*She kisses him on the cheek.*) If you wish I won't tell Raya right away about us – . This. I think – intrigue excites her.

MIKHAIL: Lydia – .

LYDIA: Please – .

MIKHAIL: You're not being fair to me!

LYDIA: I know that! This has nothing to do with fairness.

MIKHAIL: We're engaged!

LYDIA: No, we're not! Please, I don't want to miss saying goodbye to anyone. (*She stands to leave.*)

MIKHAIL: I love you. You're the only one I've ever loved.

(LYDIA *bursts out laughing – she finds that very very funny.*)

LYDIA: Now stop it. (*Beat.*) By the way, of course I'm happy you aren't dying – and I'm sure most of us feel that way.

(*She goes, the* OLD WAITER *enters. He goes to the window, he is opening a new bottle.*)

OLD WAITER: (*Drunk*) Come on! Come on! Attack! What are you waiting for?! Just start shooting!!!! (*He leaves for the restaurant.*)

SCENE 11

The restaurant. The middle of the night.

From the window – the sounds of tanks, occasional chants, voices through loud speakers, etc. There is a tension now, as the forces outside are in a stand-off. At the window, RODGERS *and* FRED. MASHA *and*

MARY *sit at the large table, though at some distance from each other.*
KATIA *and* FIODOR *sit at the small table; the* OLD WAITER *is just joining them with the newly opened bottle. Soon he will put his head down on the table and pass out. The* YOUNG WAITER *is cleaning up.*
LYDIA *stands at a distance.*

RODGERS: (*Looking out of the window*) Come on. Come on, what's taking her so long?

MARY: (*Without moving*) If you want me to see . . . ? (*She sips a drink.*) Then I won't.

FRED: If they were going to attack, why wouldn't they have done it by now?

FIODOR: You don't know what you're talking about!

FRED: I asked a question.

KATIA: Fiodor – .

FIODOR: He doesn't know what he's talking about! (*Beat.*)

FRED: (*To* RODGERS) So you were saying you know my wife.

RODGERS: We've met. I've told you. I think I've met you.

FRED: She's having our child. I wish I could be there with her.

MASHA: (*To* YOUNG WAITER) Did we get dessert? I don't think we've been offered dessert.
(*He ignores her.*)
Did we have dessert or didn't we?

KATIA: It's four thirty in the morning.

FIODOR: I'm not hungry.

KATIA: Me neither.

FIODOR: I couldn't eat –

MASHA: My point is – is he going to charge us for dessert?

KATIA: Let your father deal with – . He's paying.

FIODOR: If he lives that long. I'm not paying.

KATIA: No one asked you to – .

MASHA: Speaking of my father, has anyone seen him?

LYDIA: He'll be here soon.
(*Others turn to her, they hadn't noticed her come in. They turn back.*)
May I say something? It is my opinion that your father is a man worthy of great respect. A man to be looked up to. Honoured. I find it extraordinary that he has to pay for his own party. May I suggest that we all divide up the – .

FIODOR: I said, I'm not paying.

57

MASHA: He invited them.

(*Beat.*)

LYDIA: A good, decent – a man who has lived a full and rich life. There's something to be said for that.

(*The* OLD WAITER, *having passed out on the small table, now falls off his chair – without waking up. Others watch for a moment. He sleeps on the floor.*)

KATIA: (*To* FIODOR:) That'll be you after a couple more drinks.

(FIODOR *smiles.*)

LYDIA: Who are we waiting for?

KATIA: Natasha and Valeriy are getting a ride . . . (*Nods towards* RODGERS.)

LYDIA: To America? That's a long – .

KATIA: To the airport.

LYDIA: (*To* RODGERS) That's kind of you. (*Turns to* MASHA.) Who is he?

(MASHA *shrugs.*)

What's going on outside? Anything . . .?

RODGERS: The tanks – they're lined up in front of – .

LYDIA: (*Not listening*) Ah.

RODGERS: Some people seem to be provoking them to – .

LYDIA: (*Interrupting, holds up a drink*) Is this anyone's?

KATIA: Take it.

(LYDIA *takes the drink.*)

LYDIA: I'm so hungry, it seems like days since we ate.

MASHA: Here's some bread.

(LYDIA *takes it and eats.*)

LYDIA: When Mikhail gets here, we have an announcement.

KATIA: You're pregnant?

FIODOR: Or Raya is.

LYDIA: You'll see. But you'll have to wait.

MASHA: Where's your engagement ring? She's not wearing her – .

LYDIA: It's – .

MASHA: She's broken off her engagement!

LYDIA: I didn't say – .

MASHA: That's it, isn't it! And not a second too soon!

LYDIA: I – . (*Stops herself.*) Masha is correct, Mikhail and I are not getting married.

58

MASHA: This deserves a drink. There's a little more in the bottle – .

FIODOR: (*At the same time*) Who's he marrying – the other room-mate?

KATIA: Why can't you shut up!

FIODOR: The man's an animal – he follows his prick, he always has, he always will!

KATIA: Mikhail is a good man! And I won't sit here and listen to you attack him! If Lydia and he have made a decision, then they have very good reasons. You heard Lydia say he was a man deserving of respect! That is just how I felt about him, when we – agreed not to be married any more. I never lost my respect for him and I never will. I understand what Lydia is feeling and I think we should do the right thing and give her our greatest sympathy.

LYDIA: No, no – you don't understand, it was I who – .

KATIA: Her heart is broken! I promise you!

(MIKHAIL *has just entered with* SUSAN, *carrying her suitcase.*)

MIKHAIL: Whose heart is broken now, Katia?

KATIA: Mikhail, we just heard the news – .

(*He turns away from* KATIA *and asks* MASHA:)

MIKHAIL: What's it like outside?

MASHA: Some tanks, is that right? Someone said – .

MIKHAIL: (*Not listening, to* MARY) Look who I found struggling down the hall. (*Handing* RODGERS *the suitcase.*) Here, I gather you're all leaving.

FIODOR: (*At the same time*) Pretty strong for a dying man, I'll bet the room-mate says the same – .

(KATIA *hits him.*)

MARY: Only Susan's going now. There was only the one ticket. It's what her father wants.

(MIKHAIL *looks at her, aware that something has gone wrong.*) (*To* SUSAN) You don't mind travelling alone do you? (*Turns to* MIKHAIL.) By the way, I've tried to apologize – . I heard what – . (*To everyone*) Really, it was all my idea – he didn't know that I had . . .

MIKHAIL: Never mind.

(SUSAN *goes to* FRED. *He is a little embarrassed as she takes his arm.*)

RODGERS: I don't think we should wait.

KATIA: I'm sure they'll be here.

RODGERS: I'm sorry. We have to go.

SUSAN: (*To everyone*) Goodbye. I don't even know who you all are – but goodbye!

(*Others mumble a goodbye, nod, etc.*)

Wait. Would someone – . (*She holds up a camera.*)

RODGERS: Susan, we have to be – .

SUSAN: This will only take a second! I borrowed your camera, Grandmother. (*She puts the camera in MASHA's hands.*)

MASHA: What do I do?

SUSAN: Just push – . Thanks. (*She goes and stands with FRED, puts her arm around him. Smiling*) I love Moscow. I love it here. (*To everyone*) I can't wait to come back!

(*Picture is taken.*)

MARY: Take one of the two of us. I'd love that – .

SUSAN: We don't have time. (*Takes the camera from MASHA, goes to FRED.*) I love you. (*She kisses him, looks at him.*) Do you love me?

(*Beat.*)

FRED: (*Feeling awkward*) Of course.

(*She kisses him again and hurries off, followed by RODGERS with her suitcase.*)

MARY: Bye!

(*Pause. No one knows what to say. MIKHAIL finally goes to FRED.*)

MIKHAIL: I know what you're feeling. But there's a saying – about how girls come by like streetcars.

(*Others look at MIKHAIL in amazement. From the window, loud shouts and chanting.*)

FIODOR: I should go out there myself and knock a little sense into those hoodlums.

(*YOUNG WAITER looks at FIODOR, comes right to him, grabs a plate in front of him and leaves.*)

MASHA: I thought he was going to hit you.

FIODOR: People like that don't have the guts.

(*As the YOUNG WAITER exited, VALERIY entered with a suitcase.*)

VALERIY: Where's the man with the car?

KATIA: He just left – .

VALERIY: Wait! Goodbye, bye – ! (*Stops, and turns back, to* MARY) You – I'll send you my screenplay! (*He hurries out.*)

MARY: He doesn't have my address.

KATIA: (*After a moment*) Where's Natasha? Why isn't she with . . . ?

(MASHA *looks at* KATIA.)

MASHA: Maybe she's waiting downstairs – .

KATIA: But she didn't say goodbye!

FIODOR: With someone like that what did you expect?

(NATASHA *enters with her suitcase. She walks slowly*.)

KATIA: (*After a moment*) Valeriy just – .

MASHA: (*At the same time*) You better hurry, that American didn't seem like he would wait – .

NATASHA: I'm not in a hurry. (*She sets her suitcase down. Short pause. To* MASHA) May I stay in your apartment? I'll explain later. (*Beat.*) What's wrong? Lydia can stay with Mikhail and I'll take – .

LYDIA: We're not getting married. (*Beat.*) I'm not angry at him. In fact – I've never felt closer to him since we met. I'll explain later too.

FIODOR: Where's Raya going to sleep?

KATIA: Don't you get tired of saying the same thing over and over again? You've run that joke into the ground.

NATASHA: (*At the window*) What's happening now?

MASHA: I don't know. I don't think anyone's been paying attention.

(KATIA *stands*.)

KATIA: We're going home. I only stayed this long because I was waiting to say my goodbyes to Natasha, but now she's not going anywhere. (*To* FIODOR) Come on. I'm sure everyone will be relieved to see the last of you.

FIODOR: (*Very drunk, points to the window as he gets up*) That's been coming for a long time. Anyone could have told them. They should have asked me. Not an ounce of pity do they deserve!

(*No one has listened to him.*)

61

KATIA: Thank you, Mikhail. A lovely party. And – happy birthday. (*She kisses him and sighs.*) I'm tired.

MIKHAIL: Thank you, Katia. What would I do without you?

LYDIA: (*To* KATIA) We'll see you next week? We'll have you over to the apartment.

KATIA: That would be nice. Just us girls. (*Turns to* MARY.) Nice to meet you. What an extraordinary thing to make up. Look at him – he's as strong as a bull. (*She looks at* MIKHAIL, *fights back a tear. To* MIKHAIL) Goodbye.
(*She hurries out, followed by* FIODOR.)

FIODOR: (*As he leaves*) Everywhere you go there are Americans! I hate it!
(*They are gone.*)

LYDIA: I suppose we should too. It is very late. Natasha has to unpack.

NATASHA: And I'm sure we'll be up all night – talking. Masha, are you ready?

MASHA: (*To* MIKHAIL) Want me to see you home? I wouldn't mind.

MIKHAIL: I'm fine, Masha, thank you. (*Kisses her on the forehead.*) I have to pay the bill and . . . tip the waiters . . .
(*They look at the passed-out* OLD WAITER *on the floor.*)
You go with your friends.
(*She looks at him.*)
What??

MASHA: I'm so pleased you're not dying.

LYDIA: Is that all you're pleased about?

MASHA: What do you mean?

LYDIA: You think I didn't know how you hated the idea of Mikhail and I marrying?

MASHA: How can you say that? You're my best friend – .

NATASHA: Talk about this later. (*To* MARY) Nice to have met you. Say hello to New York for me.

FRED: I better go too – if they'll let me out. Maybe if I say I'm going home.

NATASHA: We'll talk to them at the door. Come with us. (*She takes him by the arm.*) Do you want to finish that drink?

FRED: Do you want it?

(*She takes his drink and finishes it. They look at each other.*)

LYDIA: (*To* MIKHAIL) I have a few things in your apartment. Can I come some time to pick them up?

MIKHAIL: I'll have Masha bring them to you, if that is OK with Masha.

MASHA: I don't mind. Sure. My pleasure. (*Beat.*) Goodbye.
(*Goodbyes by everyone.*)

MARY: (*Over this*) Be careful out there.
(*They hesitate, then start to leave.*)

NATASHA: (*Leaving, to* FRED) You're a businessman? You live alone?
(*They are gone. Pause.* MARY *and* MIKHAIL *are alone. The* WAITER *groans in his sleep. They look at him and then away.*)

MARY: (*Finally*) I gather they found out?
(*He nods.*)
I hope it didn't cause you any trouble. I was only trying to – .

MIKHAIL: No. No trouble at all. We all had a good laugh.

MARY: That's a relief. That's all I needed – one more thing to feel guilty about. I have enough to feel guilty about.
(*He looks at her.*)

MIKHAIL: So that is Susan.

MARY: She's upset with me. Maybe I shouldn't have called her father.

MIKHAIL: You're damned if you do and you're damned – .

MARY: Maybe he never would have found out anything. But how could I know that – you know kids, they tell everything.

MIKHAIL: They do.

MARY: Terrible liars, kids.

MIKHAIL: The worst.

MARY: So I'm the bad person! Why does it always end up this way?

MIKHAIL: But it does, doesn't it? (*Takes a bottle.*) There's a little . . .

MARY: Why not?
(*They sit and he pours. Beat.*)
They're nice. Your – wives.

MIKHAIL: They are, aren't they? All of them. I've been lucky. And at least they seemed to get along – that was my main worry – whether they would get along.

63

MARY: No, no, they . . .

(*She doesn't finish her thought. She sips her drink.*)

MIKHAIL: But I knew if I could only get them together . . .

MARY: You were right about that.

(*Short pause.*)

MIKHAIL: And of course those aren't the only women I've – . There have been many, let me tell you. I don't know how many. (*Laughs to himself.*)

MARY: I'm not surprised.

MIKHAIL: Beautiful women. Maybe – hundreds. Each one just a little different than the rest – that always amazed me. How each could be a little different. (*Beat.*) Women. (*Shakes his head and drinks. Noise from the street.*)

MARY: Sh-sh. Listen to that. Something is going to happen. You can feel it. (MARY *fights back tears.*)

MIKHAIL: (*Taking her hand*) I'm sure they'll have no problem getting to the airport. That man – he'll get her there.

MARY: (*Not listening*) I only wanted to show her – life; a life that you don't just throw away. It may not always be a nice life. It may be a hard and difficult life – full of more pain than we think a body can take – but still – you do not throw it away!

MIKHAIL: What do you mean? What are you talking about?

MARY: (*Over him*) Never mind. You couldn't understand. Thank you, I'm fine now.

(*She takes away her hand. Pause.*)

MIKHAIL: Do you want to hear something that's – I don't know, funny, I suppose.

MARY: Please. I would like that. I could use a laugh right about now.

MIKHAIL: You know – when you told my wives that I was – I was dying . . .

MARY: I now know I shouldn't have – .

MIKHAIL: What you didn't know – was that what you were telling them could – in fact, be true. (*Beat.*) Funny, isn't it?

MARY: (*Staring at him*) What do you mean? I don't understand.

MIKHAIL: Don't get upset. I said – could. I'm still waiting for the test results. The second, third test results. We think the others were – not quite correct. I'm sure I'm fine and I'll live

to a hundred and ten! (*Tries to laugh.*) Look at me, I look
great.
(MARY *covers her face.*)
I've told no one else. Not even Lydia. I didn't want to –
upset her.
(MARY *looks at him.*)
We don't know! I don't know! We're waiting for the . . .
Anyway, I suppose – thinking about all that – . It's what got
me interested in . . . (*Slaps the table.*)

MARY: Oh God!

MIKHAIL: A party seemed like a very good – . I don't know. Now
it seems stupid after – .

MARY: No, not stupid!

MIKHAIL: No one listened!

MARY: Yes they did! I did!

MIKHAIL: Not to my speech. I wrote the speech – after sixty years
of life – of a happy life though a difficult one – you have
learned a lot of things that you may wish to – . What? Pass
along? Things about life. Things people should understand.
I even had a few things I thought I would apologize for.
Especially to Katia. (*He sighs.*) If I mentioned anything at all
about the tests to them . . . I wanted them listening to me,
Misha! Not to . . .

MARY: I'm sorry then that I – .

MIKHAIL: No, no. As I said – it's funny. Now, it's funny. (*He
looks at her.*) You didn't somehow know – ? That wasn't why
you – ? I still look great.

MARY: (*As she suddenly hugs him*) You do, you do.
(*They hug.*)
(*Trying not to cry.*) I'm so sorry. I'm so sorry. I'm sorry.
(*After a moment he pulls away. Noise from the window: the
chanting of 'Yeltsin-Yeltsin-Yeltsin' can be clearly heard. He
goes to the window.*)
Mikhail?
(*He doesn't turn.*)
Mikhail? (*Beat.*) Speech. Speech. Speech.
(*He turns.*)

MIKHAIL: (*Smiling*) Thank you, but it's too – .

MARY: (*Continues, chanting now*) Speech-speech-speech-speech – .
MIKHAIL: Mary, there's no point! They're not here!
MARY: (*Banging the table*) Speech-speech-speech-speech – !
MIKHAIL: It's too late!!!
MARY: (*Banging and yelling*) Speech-speech-speech-speech – !
(*Finally, smiling, he nods. She quiets down. He moves to the head of the table, stops.*)
MIKHAIL: This is silly – .
MARY: Speech – !
MIKHAIL: OK!
(*He goes to the head of the table. He looks at her and smiles, she smiles back, never for an instant taking her eyes off him.*)
Thank you.
(*He reaches into his pocket. The* OLD WAITER *snores. They look at him and smile.* MIKHAIL *takes out his papers – unfolds them, tries to get the creases out of them, but can't. He looks at* MARY, *who stares at him. Outside the chanting continues. Finally, beginning his speech:*)
My – . My dear former – and present relatives. (*He takes a sip, clears his throat, and as he sighs*) Where – to begin?